AUTHOR

Since 2009, Chris Flaherty has written for the UK Armourer Magazine; Classic Arms & Militaria; and, Soldiers of the Queen Journal. He has advised major international museums on uniforms. For Partizan Press in 2014, he wrote and illustrated two books: 'Turkish Uniforms of the Crimean War: A Handbook of Uniforms'; and, 'The Ottoman Army in the First World War: A Handbook of Uniforms'. He co-authored and illustrated with Bruno Mugnai for Soldiershop Publishing: 2014 'Der Lange Turkenkrieg (1593-1606), Volume 1: The Long Turkish – War Habsburg Arrests the Ottoman Advance; and, in 2015 'Der Lange Turkenkrieg (1593- 1606), Volume 2: The Long Turkish War'. In 2015, he was a contributor (illustrator) to the Turkish Gallipoli Centenary Exhibition: 'From Depths to the Trenches: Gallipoli 1915', at the Isbank Museum in Istanbul. He was one of the contributors to, 'Philip Jowett, 2015 Armies of the Greek-Turkish War 1919–22', Men-at-Arms 50, Osprey Publishing. He authored a chapter on the, 'Ottoman Army in the Great Northern War' appearing in Stephen, L. Kling, Jr. (Editor) 2016 GNW Compendium: A Collection of Articles on the Great Northern War, 1700-1721 (Volume 2), The Historical Game Company. He has authored and illustrated for Partizan Press' Universal Wargames Rules Supplements: 'Napoleonic Small Siege, River Ship, Gunboat and Pontooning' (2016); 'Napoleonic Foraging, Insurrection, Marauders, Bakeries, Convoy and Encampment Wargaming' (2016); 'Napoleonic Balloon Warfare' (2017); 'Napoleonic Ottoman Army Wargaming Supplement' (2018); 'A Wargamer's Guide to WW1 Ottoman Army Uniforms' (2018); 'Napoleon's July 1798 Pyramid Campaign & the Egyptian Army' (2019); 'The Napoleonic Ottoman Army: Uniforms, Tactics and Organization' (2019). Since 2021 he has written and illustrated several titles for Soldiershop Publishing, including: 'The Sardinian Expeditionary Corps'.

PUBLISHER'S NOTES

None of unpublished images or text of our book may be reproduced in any format without the expressed written permission of Soldiershop.com when not indicate as marked with license creative commons 3.0 or 4.0. Soldiershop Publishing has made every reasonable effort to locate, contact and acknowledge rights holders and to correctly apply terms and conditions to Content. In the event that any Content infringes your rights or the rights of any third parties, or Content is not properly identified or acknowledged we would like to hear from you so we may make any necessary alterations. In this event contact: info@soldiershop.com. Our trademark: Soldiershop Publishing ©, The names of our series & brand: Museum book, Bookmoon, Soldiers&Weapons, Battlefield, War in colour, Historical Biographies, Darwin's view, Fabula, Altrastoria, Italia Storica Ebook, Witness To History, Soldiers, Weapons & Uniforms, Storia etc. are herein © by Soldiershop.com.

LICENSES COMMONS

This book may utilize part of material marked with license creative commons 3.0 or 4.0 (CC BY 4.0), (CC BY-ND 4.0), (CC BY-SA 4.0) or (CC0 1.0). Or derived from publication 70 years old or more and recolored from us. We give appropriate attribution credit and indicate if change were made in the acknowledgements field.
All our books utilize only fonts licensed under the SIL Open Font License or other free use license.

ISBN: 9791255891864 1st edition November 2024
S&W-054 - 18th CENTURY JANISSARY, ARTILLERY AND SAPPERS - VOLUME 2
Written and illustrated by Chris Flaherty
Editor: Luca Cristini Editore, for the brand: Soldiershop. Cover & Art Design: Luca S. Cristini.

CHRIS FLAHERTY

18ᵀᴴ CENTURY JANISSARY, ARTILLERY AND SAPPERS

UNIFORMS, TACTICS AND ORGANIZATION VOLUME 2

SOLDIERS&WEAPONS 054

CONTENTS & INTRODUCTION

Following from Volume I on uniforms, badges and rank insignia for 18th Century Turkish and other European Janissary, Volume II looks at Janissary organization and tactics used in battle by the Turkish Kapikulu Ocaklari [Kapikulu Akerleri]: Standing Army, from the later 18th Century to the Napoleonic era, and the traditional Artillery, Miners and Transport Troops, that had a direct relationship in terms of entrenchment battle tactics used at the time. This volume also looks at Religious Officials and the regulation of organization, weapons, tactics and uniforms; Orta Imam, Saka and Medical support; Mehtar and Turkish Music Soldiers in European armies generally.

Chapter 1: Janissary Organization..5

Chapter 2: Janissary Weapons and Equipment................................11

Chapter 3: Janissary Camps...17

Chapter 4: Entrenched Battle and Janissary Tactics......................21

Chapter 5: Traditional Artillery..34

Chapter 6: Artillery Uniforms..42

Chapter 7: Artillery Tactics..45

Chapter 8: Legamdji, Cebeci and Arabaci..50

Chapter 9: Religious Officials and Religious Regulation.............53

Chapter 10: Orta Imam, Saka and Medical Support.......................56

Chapter 11: Mehtar and Turkish Music Soldiers in European Armies......60

REFERENCES..67

CHAPTER 1: JANISSARY ORGANIZATION

In the late 18th Century, the Turkish Army size was reputed to be large, "[the]... collected force of the Empire is said to amount to 400,000 Soldiers."[1] However, a survey of the military's actual strength only counted some 186,400, "effective men"[2]. In the case of Janissary institutionally, its vast numbers represented a social welfare system:

> "a muster roll of close to half a million men, who were paid a fee per man. Probably 1 in 10 were actual fighting forces."[3]

It is known, by 1761 the Kapikulu Ocaklari: Standing Army[4], also known to have been called the Kapikulu Akerleri: Sultan's Army, during the 15th to 17th Centuries[5], had 55,731 Soldiers registered for use in campaign, which had been progressively falling since the start of the 18th Century[6]. It has been stated, by the late 18th Century, the: "Empire was only capable of raising 30,000 troops for a major campaign."[7] These troops represented, "Janissary, Artillerists, and Gun-Carriage Drivers"[8].

THE JANISSARY ORTA

Janissary Orta in the 18th Century, operated in a much different way than a European Infantry Regiment, of the same period, that generally came into being around the late 17th Century. For this reason, the description, "Chambers"[9], is given to describe the Janissary Orta; and in the Napoleonic period, the size of these organizations varied significantly: "The number of men composing each ... [Orta] ... varies, and is not limited; for, in general, that ... [Orta] ... which has gained the greatest renown in war exploits is sought after by those who wish to enlist."[10] By the Napoleonic period, the size of the Orta organization had reached unmanageable proportions:

> "The number of ... [Janissary] ... in each... [Orta] ... is not fixed, but depends upon its celebrity; from a vanity natural enough, greater numbers enrolling themselves in such ... [Orta] ... as are most distinguished; the number in some is extremely great, that of the thirty-fifth, amounting to nearly thirty thousand."[11]

However, a 1798 survey of the actual strength of the Turkish Army , recorded some 113,400 militarily active Janissary[12]. Distributing this total number among the 101 traditional Orta would have given each of these up to 1,200 or so. It is known only a select number of Janissary was ready for combat at any time: "When the Grand Vizier assembles an Army, the different ... [Pasha] ... choose out such of the ... [Janissary] ... in their respective provinces as are fittest for the campaign, register

---

1 McLean, 1818.
2 Eton, 1798.
3 Aksan, 2002.
4 Uyar, 2009.
5 Nicolle, 1995.
6 Agoston, 2011.
7 Nicolle, 1998.
8 Agoston, 2011.
9 Morier, 1801.
10 Morier, 1801.
11 McLean, 1818.
12 Eton, 1798.

their names, order them an allowance for their journey, and send them to join the Army"[13]. There is also a reference, from around the 1740s where a Janissary could be censured for bad behaviour and one of the punishments was being marked-out for, "dangerous assignments on campaign."[14]

ODAS: BARRACKS COMPANIES

The Janissary Orta appears to have had a Company sub-structure composed of sub-units: called Odas. These generally numbered up to 130 each[15][16]. Odas are generally understood to be, "Barracks Companies"[17].

BOLUKS: SUB-DIVISIONS

The 61 Boluk Orta constituted the Second Division of Janissary. It is known that several Odas composed a Boluk [Ocak]: Regiment numbering 1,000[18][19]. Some Barracks Rooms: Odas, were referred to as Boluk [Buluk]: Files (Sub-Regiments) of Artillery, and the Arabaci: Wagoners.

DISBANDED ORTA

All Janissary enrolled in one of the Orta. However, not all original Orta still existed by the 18th Century. For instance, the 64th and 65th Cemaat Janissary Cavalry Orta, called the Zagarczs: Grey Hound Keepers (as they were originally part of the Sultan's hunting establishment), were suppressed by Sultan Murad IV, in 1623, for involvement in the murder of Sultan Osman II. After disbandment, it is known: "The number sixty-five was left vacant, and a solemn curse was pronounced upon it at every weekly distribution of candles to the barracks of the ... [Janissary]."[20]

IMPERIAL JANISSARY REGIMENTS

The Grand Vizier's Army, in Egypt, in 1800 had 13,000 Janissary, who appear to have been organized into four major contingents, from those raised in Europe, and those, "raised in Syria for the garrisons of Aleppo, Damascus, and Cairo"[21]; who were likely Imperial Janissary Regiments. Janissary sent to major city garrisons, would double-enroll in the local Imperial Janissary Regiments, which were part of the Province Governors' Army. An Imperial Janissary Regiment had a separate identity from the original Orta that the Janissary who made up these came from (and remained enrolled in). In some cases, the Imperial Janissary Regiment had different local organization from that found elsewhere. For instance, in the late 18th Century, the Tunisia Imperial Janissary Corps, had its Janissary allotted into units: Orta (or room) of 20 to 25 Soldiers in active service, with an additional 30 or more pensioners[22]. In the 1680s, there is a mention of the, "standard provinces contributing forces, elite units from Egypt, Aleppo, and Damascus, numbering 3,000, 1,500 and 1,500 respectively[23]. A reference to the Aleppo Janissary Garrison, during Napoleon's invasion of Syria,

---

13 McLean, 1818.
14 Barbir, 2014.
15 Johnson, 1988.
16 Johnson, 1988.
17 Hathaway, 2002.
18 Hathaway, 2002.
19 Moalla, 2005.
20 Tyrrell, 1910.
21 Morier, 1801.
22 Moalla, 2005.
23 Uyar, 2009.

states, "the city's Janissary fought as a separate contingent."[24] An English journal from the Egyptian campaign mentions the, "corps of Turks, under Ibrahim … [Pasha] … of Aleppo", and that it had 2,000 Soldiers[25]. There is also a 1799 account from an English traveler who calculated that the full garrison in Aleppo, there were only 15,000 Janissary, and while had, "superior valour … [they were] … little acquainted with the use of arms or aspect of battle."[26]

The smaller of the Janissary contingents in the Egyptian campaign was that from Damascus. Traditionally, in the 16th and 17th Centuries, the Damascus Janissary were horse mounted on the march. One of the main roles of the Damascus garrison, known as the Yerli: Local Janissary[27], was to provide fort garrisons comprising 12 to 50 Soldiers along the pilgrimage caravan route[28]. The Commander of these forts was an, "Odabashi … [Odabasi] … chosen from among the Janissary of Damascus."[29] Damascus Janissary might not have been a large unit, as in 1708, "an inspection of local Janissary muster roles … found that, of 1,231 members of the Corps, the majority were unfit for service because they were either too old and feeble or underage"[30]. Following this review, "numbers were reduced to 913 (of whom 35 were pensioners) … distributed through eight Cavalry units (Cemaat) and forty-two Companies (Boluk) of Foot Soldiers."[31] This corps was further reduced to 720 men by 1720. The Damascus garrison was also unusual, in that there was a second corps, since 1660 called the Imperial Janissary. In 1740, it was known that there were, "two Ortas (Companies) of Imperial Janissary"[32]. It may be the case, that as Companies these were the small Janissary Odas: Sub-Units. The military effectiveness of the two Corps of Janissary in Damascus was likely open to question. It is known, by 1806 the city garrison, and the Imperial Janissary, had constantly feuded for decades[33]. It appears, actual military service, apart from protecting the pilgrimage route, by the mid-18th Century was rarely experienced[34][35]. It is also known, some of the Janissary from the Damascus garrison may have ended up in French service, as a unit of Syrian Janissary Infantry was formed in 1799.

In Egypt, the Army had traditionally been composed of seven Ojaqs [Odjacklis]: Militia Regiments, and that by 1797, these had 18,000 Soldiers[36]. Egyptian Ojaqs: Regiments were led by a Bas Bug: Commander, who ranked as an Agha; and by Zabits: Regimental Officers. One of the Egyptian Ojaqs [Odjacklis] was an Imperial Janissary Regiment that had been based in Cairo since the 16th Century[37][38]. This unit of Janissary was known to have been traditionally horse mounted on the march, during the 16th and 17th Centuries. A 1798 survey of the actual strength of the Turkish Army, records a unit of 3,000 Infantry and Cavalry from Egypt called the, Messirlis[39]. This unit is more typically known as the Mustahfizan: Guards[40][41][42], or "the Guardians"[43]. The Cairo Mustahfizan was,

---

24 Hathaway, 2014.
25 Walsh, 1803.
26 Browne, 1799.
27 Douwes, 2000.
28 Barbir, 2014.
29 Burckhardt, 1822.
30 Barbir, 2014.
31 Barbir, 2014.
32 Barbir, 2014.
33 Grehan, 2007.
34 Douwes, 2000.
35 Barbir, 2014.
36 Ozturk, 2016.
37 Walsh, 1803.
38 Ozturk, 2016.
39 Eton, 1798.
40 Winter, 2003.
41 Fuccaro, 2016.
42 Ozturk, 2016.
43 Damurdashi, 1991.

"by far the largest of Egypt's Regiments, numbering several thousand by the end of the Eighteenth Century."[44] A 1797 return lists the Regiments' strength as 6,893 Soldiers[45]. It is known, that this unit, "were … on call for military expeditions within Egypt and comprised the bulk of the Governor's contribution to imperial campaigns."[46] There is also a reference, in Egypt, to a Regiment called the Mutafarriqa[47]; also called the Muteferrika[48]. Mutafarriqa numbered in 1797 some 1,519 Soldiers. Composed of both Infantry and Cavalry and were a, "prestigious Regiment", attached to the Governor's Council: Divan[49]. It is possible that the Mutafarriqa was a sub-unit of the Cairo Mustahfizan and represented the militarily active enrollees only.

WARTIME AD-HOC JANISSARY ORTA-BATTALIONS

Turkish authorities are known to have created ad-hoc Janissary Wartime Regiments, or Orta-Battalions on a regular basis. All active Janissary in Constantinople were expected to report for service. During the Russian-Turkish War of 1809 till 1812, there is mention of organizing new Janissary Regiments[50]. These new Regiments appear to have been composite units composed of volunteers from various Orta and allotted to the wartime units. Some of these may have been solely composed of Janissary from the same Orta; however, many were likely mixed units. Mention is made of the loss of five Janissary Regiments taken as prisoners by the Russians, in the summer of 1811. In April 1812, there is mention of three Janissary Regiments from Constantinople, consisting of 3,000 Soldiers, who were ordered to join the Field Army. Units such as these suggest standard Foot units of Musketeers organized into Orta-Battalions, typically numbering about 1,000 Soldiers. Modern historians give greater numbers, for an Orta operating as a field Battalion, by the time of Sultan Selim III, "a tactical unit numbering about 2,000 to 3,000 troops."[51] This may not be reliable, as an account from Egypt in 1800, indicates much smaller standard units of about 1,000 Soldiers each: "two Regiments of 200 men each deserted for no other reason, than that the Grand Vizier refused to pay them as if they had their full complement of 1,000"[52]. The standard field commander for an Orta: Battalion was a Bimbashi: Leader of a Thousand.

ECONOMIC JANISSARY

Among Janissary ranks there were a great many more Senior Level Officers who are usually seen as largely Administrative Officials. These Officers likely had little in the way of a direct military function. The role of these Officers is seen by modern historians as somehow equivalent to modern-day Company and Regimental Clerical Officers. This is also a misinterpretation, as Janissary by the 18th Century had institutionally amassed a vast economic portfolio of business interests, and holdings dominating the Empires' economy[53]. It is known, that by the 17th and 18th Centuries, "selling Janissary certificates that enabled their holders to draw pay and receive daily food rations … became a lucrative business for Officers and bureaucrats."[54]

---

44 Hathaway, 2002.
45 Damurdashi, 1991.
46 Hathaway, 2002.
47 Damurdashi, 1991.
48 Hathaway, 2002.
49 Hathaway, 2002.
50 Sunar, 2006.
51 Johnson, 1988.
52 Walsh, 1803.
53 Sunar, 2006.
54 Agoston, 2011.

▶ A small alloy brass-copper disk, some 3 by 2½ centimeters engraved with the word 'Janissary'[55]. Likely from the later 18th Century, it is believed it was used by an Economic Janissary to identify themselves to other Janissary for protection.

The Janissary business empire led to the massive influx of Economic Janissary who were not Soldiers but tradesmen who joined various Orta for business reasons. By the 18th Century, entry into the Janissary had been opened to enrolled men who, "[practiced] ... the lowest trades ... [and had] ... nothing military but the name Janissary"[56]. By enrolling in various Orta, tradesmen could secure their business activities[57]. Economic Janissary would display their Orta badge over business premises[58].

It is not known how far Economic Janissary were inducted, if at all, into military life. However, in the case of the Rumeli Janissary, who were largely Economic Janissary, who had come about through, "enrolment of Muslim artisans in the Janissary Corps ... [that] ... gave them status, including the right to bear arms."[59]

ZTRHLI NEFER FOOT SOLDIERS

Janissary committing a significant deed on the battlefield, such as surviving near suicidal missions, could be promoted to the Sultan's Household Guard Kapikulu Sipahi and Silahtar Cavalry Regiments. Traditionally, joining the Ztrhli Nefer was a status given to ordinary Janissary released from their Orta. Nicknames commonly given to the Ztrhli Nefer because of their unusual, almost suicidal and courageous battle tactics, included: Serdengectiler: Head Givers; meaning: 'the one who has already given his head to the enemy' (one who does not care if he lived or died); were often used to describe the Janissary undertaking this work. Traditionally, a small unit of armour-clad Infantry Soldiers are known to have been used in battles, and operated in small 30 to 100 strong bands of hand-picked Soldiers. Wearing the best and heaviest armour, including the round iron-steel plate shield. Primarily used during sieges, on the open battlefield, they were tasked with storming enemy strong points and breaches in the walls, often under the cover of darkness using stealth and surprise. It is known by the Napoleonic period, the phrase – Serdengecti, had somewhat changed its meaning or use, "[by the] ... late Eighteenth and Early Nineteenth Century ... the term was simply employed to describe the Janissary volunteers for campaigns"[60].

---

55 Yener, 2017.
56 Eton, 1798.
57 Sunar, 2006.
58 Sunar, 2006.
59 Sadat, 1972.
60 Sunar, 2006.

INDIVIDUAL WARRIORS SEEKING MARTYRDOM

A 1787 account from the Russian-Turkish War states how Turkish troops were,

> "roused almost to madness by their enraged ... [Imam] ... who mingled in the battle, and excited ... [them] ... to the combat. These men became the martyrs of their zeal, and the death they inflamed others to seek, they themselves found."[61]

▲ A somewhat allegorical period illustration is known, from the early 1830s, which depicts French troops fighting at the gates of Algiers[62]. Illustrating a somewhat peculiar scene, namely a small number of sword armed semi-naked warriors rushing towards the French, armed only with swords. Cloaks pulled around their heads, appears to suggest individual Warriors seeking martyrdom, as they appear in traditional white cotton or linen cloth burial shrouds. The illustration shows the attacking Warriors wearing small loincloths, which may be a period addition to not show nudity. Instances of the tradition of 'holy fools' in society and nudity, and semi-nudity are known: "wandering the street naked or wearing only a loincloth were two ... [of the] ... distinctive practices adopted by many, although by no means all, male holy fools."[63] Traditionally, one of the ways that a person might attain public recognition that they were divinely blessed, was the demonstration of: "Supranormal physical qualities ... such as apparent invulnerability of indifference to the elements."[64]

---

61 Anthing, 1813.
62 Unknown, 1830.
63 Scalenghe, 2014.
64 Scalenghe, 2014.

CHAPTER 2: JANISSARY WEAPONS AND EQUIPMENT

Presenting a strikingly different appearance to the European Soldiers' load equipment of the period, the Janissary was equipped more like a huntsman, commonly seen in Europe, carrying a musket, hanger sword, ammunition bag, powder horn and other weapons tucked into the belt. Traditionally, Janissary only ever saw weapons when they were training, or preparing for a battle; other than that, they marched unarmed, transporting all their firearms by wagon. Historically, Janissary primarily fought as Light Infantry and traditionally had been bow armed. By the 18th Century, in addition to muskets individual Janissary carried a variety of personal weapons. Period commentators frequently refer to wearing waist bands or sashes, usually in red cloth, used to carry additional weapons such as pistols and knives. This basic equipment set had not changed, even in the Napoleonic period; an English Diplomat who observed the Janissary's uniform: "Besides a musket, they carry a pair of pistols and a large knife, which are fastened to their waist by a sash."[65]

MUSKETS

After 1558, it is known, Janissary were increasingly free to buy their own muskets from imported gun makers. It is said that: "[Turkish] … musket-barrels are much esteemed; but they are too heavy … they are … made round a rod of iron they twist soft old iron wire, and forge it; then they bore out the rod, part of which often remains, according as the wire was thick or thin, and the bore large or small."[66] Traditionally, "muskets shot larger balls, had a longer range with more penetrating power compared to other European muskets"[67]. It was known that, "Turkish sniper-fire … [was] … said to be more accurate than European ones … from over 500 feet range made rampart sentry walk untenable."[68] Tufenk: matchlock was known to be longer barreled, with a heavier ball shot[69]. During the earlier Long War (in the 1600s), and still likely the case in the early 18th Century, Janissary firearms fired bullets of 12 to15 grams; which approximately translated to gun calibres of 13 to 14 millimeters. These muskets were 115 to 140 centimeters long, and weighed 3 to 4.5 kilograms each[70]. In the 18th Century, "most … [Janissary] … Tufenk (muskets) were matchlocks rather than the newer flintlocks."[71] In the 18th Century, Turkish also used a flintlock musket: Muskat Tufenkleri with a strong European influence in its design[72]. These muskets were also distinctive, a description of these weapons used by the Albanian troops in Egypt: "Their firearms are in general beautifully ornamented in silver and gold; their muskets are light, and are made like a tomahawk at the but-end, I imagine to be used in self-defence in cases of necessity."[73]

---

65 Morier, 1801.
66 Eton, 1798.
67 Sakul, 2013.
68 Gush, 1975.
69 Nicolle, 1995.
70 Agoston, 2005.
71 Nicolle, 1998.
72 Nicolle, 1995.
73 Morier, 1801.

RIFLED MUSKETS

Rifled types of muskets are known to have been used by the Janissary[74]. The rifled musket had an early introduction to the Janissary and Mameluke of Egypt, originating from the Balkan region, these typically had seven grooved barrels[75]. In Egypt, in 1800, it was noted by a British observer that Janissary,

> "carry a short rifle-barrel musket, flung across the shoulder, without a bayonet. The fire of these muskets, the greater part of which are manufactured at Damascus, cannot be very brisk, as they require a considerable time to load."[76]

POWDER HORN AND BLACK POWDER CHARGE BOTTLES

Janissary powder horns are commonly seen looping onto their belt[77]. Janissary do not appear to have favored the use of paper cartridges. An 1805 illustration of a Janissary in full dress[78], shows an ordinary cross belt for the ammunition bag, while another 1805 illustration of an Egyptian Janissary[79], shows several black powder charge bottles hanging from the carry strap, and this may be illustrative as to the amount of prepared ammunition carried. There is a reference to cloth ammunition loops, attached as breast cartridge pouches of a type classically seen as later Cossack items of dress, from an account during the 1770s Russian-Turkish War, noting due to rain which soaked the Turkish uniforms, "as they used small pockets, instead of cartridge-boxes, their powder was moistened, and rendered unfit for use."[80] Two matching red velvet and silver tape ammunition bandolier belt pads – one is said to be 19th Century Greek, the other Persian[81]; however, more likely Turkish in origin, have several individual pockets for inserting silver musket cartridge bottles, with tops connected by attachment chains. These powder charge pouch pads slipped onto a silver tape cloth belt.

AMMUNITION BAG AND BOX

The amount of ammunition carried by a Janissary Musketeer may have been substantial. Typically, in 1598, for example, the Janissary is said to have been issued some 300 balls, and sufficient powder for their individual firearms before a battle. A full issue of 300 rounds does sound excessive. However, it needs to be recognized Turkish tended to prefer fighting from static defensive entrenchments. Notwithstanding, 300 rounds represent a considerable weight of metal being carried by each Soldier on the battlefield. Based on the typical musket ball weight it can be suggested each Janissary carried at least 4.2 kilograms of lead balls in their ammunition bag, slung over the shoulders on a carry strap, or looped on their belt[82]. A large ammunition pouch-box slung on its cross-strap is seen in a picture of Artillery Drivers[83]. Several illustrations show Turkish troops with cross-belts seen from

---

74 Nicolle, 1995.
75 Elgood, 1995.
76 Wittman, 1803.
77 Knotel, 1890.
78 Unknown, 1805.
79 Unknown, 1805.
80 Anthing, 1813.
81 Laking, 1964.
82 Knotel, 1890.
83 Unknown, 1805.

the front only[84]. One 1803 dated illustration shows a small ammunition box hanging at the back of several Turkish Soldiers, directly under the waist sash[85]. It is possible these are Russian items taken and used from the battlefield.

SPEAR BAYONET

Janissary were said to be opposed to using the bayonet, which was likely more a cause celebre. Historically, it has been argued that throughout the late 17th, and 18th Centuries, "[Turkish] … Soldiers … rejected the use of the pike and … [later] … the bayonet as 'infidel arms', and their objection … was expressed in cultural-religious terms."[86] In regards to pike use, it appears this weapon was initially used by Janissary in the age of Sultan Suleyman [Suleiman I] the magnificent (1520 till 1566). By the time of Sultan Mahomet IV (1648 till 1687) the Janissary, "had given up the use of the pike"[87]. There appears to have been two short-lived attempts to introduce bayonets, said to have been, "in 1738 … then dropped and taken up again in 1755"[88]. Little is known about the use of these weapons except these were listed as part of the weapons of the Janissary from a stocktaking in the Museum of St. Irene, in Constantinople, and the dates coincide with known attempts at military reform[89].

The only image we have of a Janissary armed with a musket and bayonet, is that of the 1770 Polish Janissary[90]. This shows the right-angle bar is longer, connecting to a socket-tube. The blade appears to be a broad leaf, resembling a spear, and much shorter, possibly even being a converted spearhead.

▶ 1770 Polish Janissary Spear Bayonet.

HAND GRENADES

It is recorded that the Cebehane: Imperial Ammunition House distributed grenades to troops during campaigns. Janissary used hand grenades during siege operations[91]. The Elkumbarasi: Gunpowder Hand Grenade was common from 1560. Early Turkish gunpowder hand grenades with an earthenware body, were used after the 1560s[92]. Later iron grenades were used[93]. In 1678, the Cebehane had 23,520 grenades, and between 1687, and 1689, some 164,000 grenades, using two types: 126,500 Tane-Ihumbara-Ideste: Regular Iron Grenades; and, 37,484 Sise-Ihumbara-Ideste: Glass Grenades[94]. Usually thrown by hand, the grenades could also be fired from a specially designed musket.

---

84 Hochenleitter, 1788.
85 Wittman, 1803.
86 Levy, 1982.
87 Creasy, 1878.
88 Brill, 1913.
89 Levy, 1982.
90 Le Prince, 1770.
91 Agoston, 2005.
92 Uyar, 2009.
93 Mugnai, 2014.
94 Agoston, 2005.

HANGER SWORD AND KILIJ: CURVE-BLADED SCIMITAR-SWORD

Turkish Soldiers in the 18th Century wore a variety of European hanger swords, alongside the famed Kilij: curve-bladed scimitar-sword. Often called the, "Damascus scimitar"[95]. Kilij after 1750 were rarely made from patterned-forged Wootz Steel, which had made these sword blades famous for their tough, shatter resistant and extremely sharp edges. By the late 18th Century, Kilij were shortened to a typical overall length of 27 inches, the blade itself formed into an acute curve. The first two-thirds of the blade had a narrow width, while the last-third of its length (towards its point), called the Yalman: the blade flared, and was much wider. This feature was said to greatly add to the swords' cutting power. The back of the blade had a distinct 'T-shaped' cross section that allowed for greater blade stiffness without increasing its weight. The distinctive shape of the blade around its tip allows a thrust movement to be performed, in addition to the typical sabre sweep-action, or slicing cut. Kilij when compared to European sabres, it was said: "the edge of … [European] … sabres … [were] … never sharp enough, and the angle of the edge is too acute."[96] The Turkish weapon in comparison had a much thicker blade, with a broader edge. It is known, that the Kilij: "have one great defect, brittleness; they are apt to fly like glass by a blow given injudiciously, though a person used to cut with them will, without any danger of breaking … or turning its edge, cut through an iron nail as thick as a man's finger."[97] It is interesting to note, illustrations show the swords slung in their scabbards with the blade uppermost[98], a technique used to preserve the blade-edge from wear to keep its sharpness. The wooden scabbard was leather covered with brass fittings. Carry cords attached to the scabbard rings.

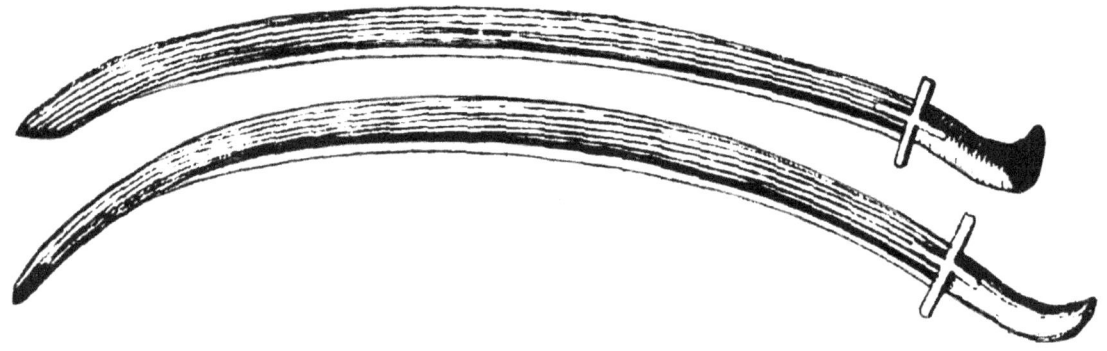

▲ A 1732 illustration of Turkish Kilij[99].

▶ A heavy version of the Turkish grenade firing musket, along with a possible reconstruction of the so-called 'Abusgun', which is said to have been used by Turkish Soldiers prior to the introduction of the conventional howitzer in the 17th Century, which are also known as the Abus [Obus]. It was supposed to have been supported on a tripod frame. It appears to have been used by the Artillery Infantry to protect their Battery from attack.

---

95 Alison, 1840.
96 Eton, 1798.
97 Eton, 1798.
98 Sevket, 1907.
99 Marsigli, 1732.

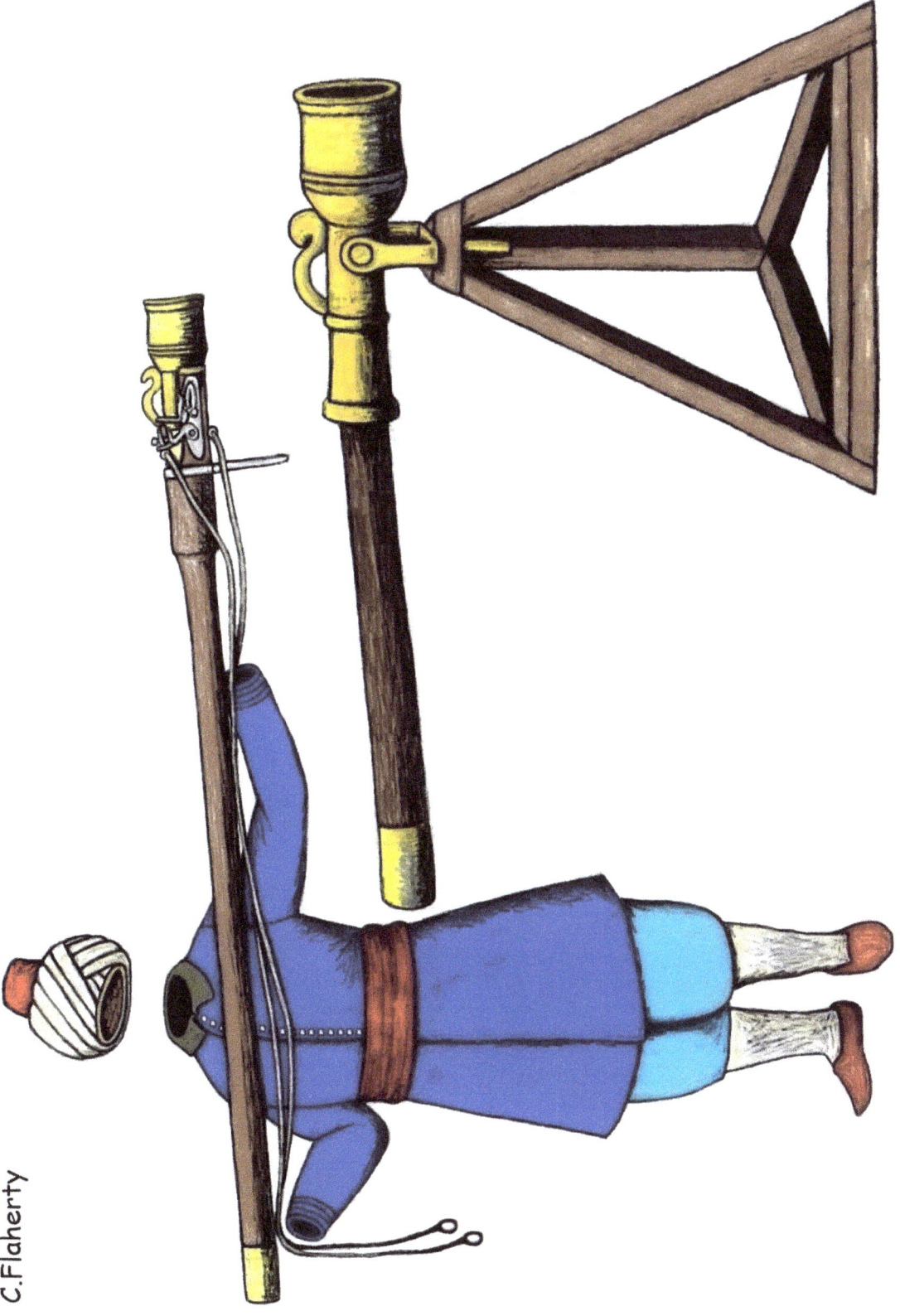

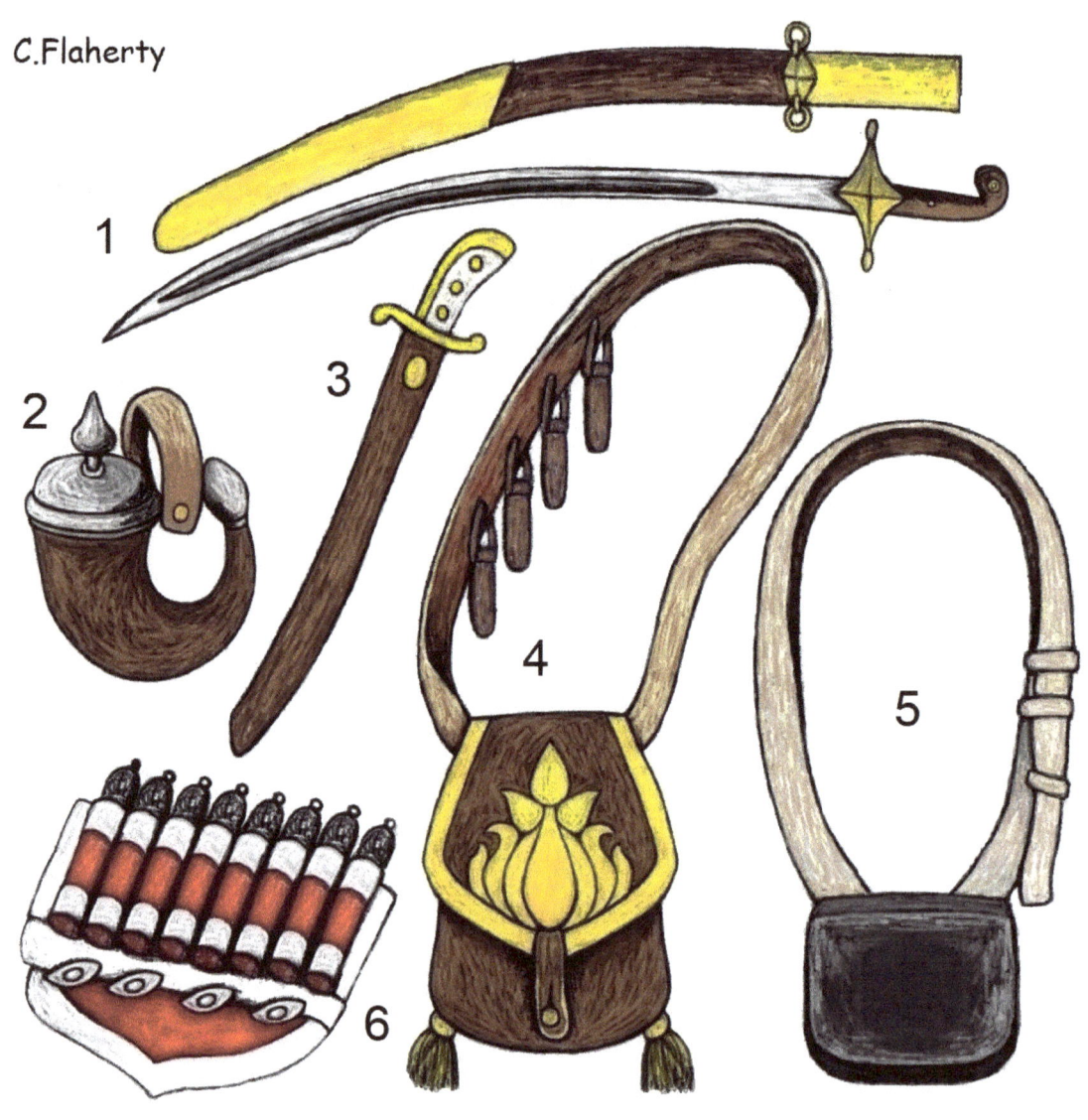

FIGURE 1: Kilij and scabbard.
FIGURE 2: Powder horn.
FIGURE 3: Hanger sword.
FIGURE 4: Ammunition bag and bandolier belt, with hanging ammunition-bottles.
FIGURE 5: Ammunition box on carry strap.
FIGURE 6: Ammunition-bottles looped pad worn on a belt.

CHAPTER 3: JANISSARY CAMPS

Turkish Soldiers did not appear to have adopted a regular plan to their camps: "The tents, which are of different colours and shapes, were irregularly strewed over a space of ground several miles in circuit"[100]. However, a survey of the military's actual strength does list a force of 6,000 who were part of the Army, called the, "Mehtergees, who erect the tents and place the camp"[101]. It was also the case, that many Soldiers likely camped, as they arrived from the march,

> "a very ingenious definition of it was given by a Turk, who was asked to describe their manner of encampment. Thus, said he, pulling from his pocket a handful of … [coins] … and throwing them carelessly on a table."[102]

An English account of the Egyptian campaign describes the main camp:

> "The Grand Vizier's Army arrived on the other side of the Nile, nearly opposite to us, and a great multitude they appeared to be. With tents and marquees pitched without order, camels, horses, asses, Arabs, they covered a great extent of ground. There was little subordination or regularity among them."[103]

The English diplomat with the Turkish Army in Egypt, described as the,

> "only principle is, that the different corps, or nations, of which this heterogeneous body is composed, have their several encampments. But if there happen to be two leaders, commanding each a separate detachment of the same class of troops, both pitch their tents where they please: the tent of the chief stands in the midst of those of his followers"[104].

However, there was order to the camp, as it is generally known, that the, "Grand Vizier's huge, richly embroidered tent was pitched in the centre of the Janissary, themselves at the heart of the camp"[105]. Along with Janissary pavilion-tents, which served the function of Orta insignia, tents for ordinary Janissary are described as, "different colours and shapes."[106] In the case of the tent of the Turkish Grand Bashaw [Pasha]: Admiral and General in Egypt, in 1800:

> "which for grandeur surpassed anything of the kind I ever saw. The marque was covered with red velvet lined with blue, gold tassels and fringes."[107]

It is known the tent of a Seraskier: Commander-in-Chief: Pasha of two, or three, horse-tails, was green[108]. Another account of the Turkish encampment in Egypt, stated, "[the] … Grand Vizier generally chooses a height for his tent, which may be distinguished by a wall of cloth that surrounds

---

100 Morier, 1801
101 Eton, 1798.
102 Morier, 1801.
103 Low, 1911.
104 Morier, 1801.
105 Aksan, 2002.
106 Morier, 1801.
107 Low, 1911.
108 McLean, 1818.

▲ Based on a 1732 illustration showing the camp layout with its tents arranged in groups around an Orta commander's tent with the Kazan cooking pot. A surrounding ditch with timber bridges at regular intervals is used as a trench for Janissary to fight from with heavy and light-swivel cannons inside or overhead behind the trench line.

it"[109]. One account describes tent interiors, for the higher serving elites: "They were lodged in spacious tents, divided into several apartments, the insides lined with rich stuffs, and the bottom covered with beautiful ... [Turkish] ... carpets."[110] A 1789 account of the Russian-Turkish War provides a description of the camp of the Grand Vizier, "considerable riches were found there, together with the large and superb tent of that Generalissimo, the interior of which was almost entirely of cloth of gold and silver."[111] In addition to the Grand Vizier's tent, this was surrounded by those of his, "own attendants, the members of his household, and domestics, encamp about him, and form his Bodyguard"[112]. Tents of a lower-level Pasha were, "distinguished by a silver ball which is fixed to the tent pole, and by the standards, with the number of horse-tails denoting his rank, planted before his tent."[113] A further distinction of the Pasha's tents included lit torches:

> "A Turkish camp is lighted up at night by a kind of large lanterns, formed of iron hoops, and fastened upon long poles. Several of these lights, in which rags impregnated with grease, oil, or a resinous substance, are burned, are placed in the front of the tent of each of the ... [Pasha]."[114]

Along with the camp tents that had to be transported, all the furnishings that went with these also had to be carried out on campaign. An English Diplomat's account; during the Egyptian campaign, records how the Army's pack camels on a march through the desert transported: "Commodious ... [sofas] ... tents, beds, pipes, and all descriptions of Eastern luxuries, were a greater object; and, rather than make a sacrifice to their ideas of grandeur, an Army was to risk perishing."[115] It is known,

---

109 Morier, 1801.
110 Walsh, 1803.
111 Anthing, 1813.
112 Morier, 1801.
113 Morier, 1801.
114 Wittman, 1803.
115 Morier, 1801.

throughout the 16th and 17th Centuries, the Camel Drivers were primarily used as part of the transport train[116]. An English Diplomat's account from the Turkish Army in Egypt, recorded that its train consisted of 40,000 pack camels[117].

In front of the Orta commander's tent there was a Kazan: cooking pot used to issue daily ration of pilau: porridge given to the Janissary[118]. A 17th Century chronicle describes each Soldier had an Agha: small wooden bowl, used for collecting their food rations and eating from. A Turkish account describes how Janissary and Levend on the warships at the Golden Horn, in Constantinople unhappy with their rations protested by throwing their personal bowls into the water[119]. A large cooking tray was also shared between a group, eating communally with their hands, or wooden spoons[120]. This practice was still being seen in WW1, in the Turkish Army, where, "a copper cooking dish … [was issued] … to every ten men"[121]. A 1917 photograph, titled: "The daily soup ration", shows eight Turkish Soldiers around a cooking dish about to eat from it with their spoons[122].

CAMP SECURITY

Turkish Soldiers on the march simply camped and did not entrench, and this was a source of confusion to contemporary observers. An English diplomat, who accompanied the Turkish Army in Egypt, arrived at its march camp at night, entering it without being stopped; remarking - highly critical of camp security in general: "None of the precautions that are thought necessary to prevent surprise in armies much better able to withstand a sudden attack, are even thought of in a Turkish Army."[123] There is an account from the opening of the Russian-Turkish War, of an incident occurring at the camp covering Khotyn [Khotin; Cbocim]; recorded as a Russian victory, where the Turkish Army was said to have taken heavy casualties; one of the English observers critical of the lack of security in camps, he saw in Egypt, recounted this story:

> "The dreadful massacre which occurred on the 17th of September, 1769, arose from the unprepared state of fourteen thousand Turks encamped, and the very feeble resistance they were in consequence enabled to make. Instead of defending themselves, the greater part of them crept under the tents, where they were put to death by the bayonet, without imploring the mercy of their vanquishers."[124]

Weakness in camp security was recognized under the military reform of Sultan Selim III, as he made the Nizam-i Cedit: New Order Army adopt the use of a watchword, like that used in the Russian Army, to stop the infiltration of spies into the Army camp, as commonly no system of passwords was employed by the Turkish Army[125]. Traditionally, it should be noted that encampment security was in the hands of the 19th Boluk Janissary Orta, known as the Bekci: Sentinels, who formed the Army's Guards on campaign, and had a tattoo of a standing tree. In general, it was only in the face of the enemy that the Turkish Army would begin to entrench expecting a battle to follow.

---

116 Uyar, 2009.
117 Morier, 1801.
118 Marsigli, 1732.
119 Omer, 1807.
120 Walsh, 1803.
121 British General Staff, 1995.
122 Library of Congress.
123 Morier, 1801.
124 Wittman, 1803.
125 Sakul, 2009.

CAMP DOG KEEPERS

▼ 71st Cemaat Janissary Orta dog tattoo.

Some English observers of the Turkish Army in Egypt mention stray dogs in camps, and traditionally, two of the Senior Officers who served the Grand Vizier, were the Samsoongis Bashi: Principal Dog-Keeper, and the Zahergis Bashi: Secondary Dog-Keeper[126]. The role of these Officers, related to how, "originally, a certain number of dogs were, in a Turkish Army, attached to the troops; but this practice having been long discontinued ... [by the Napoleonic period]"[127]. Military use of dogs continued in Egypt, and as late as 1714 there are references to the use of trained dogs to secure unattended places[128].

The traditional role of Soldier Dog Keepers was represented by the 64th Cemaat Janissary Cavalry Orta, called the Zagarczs: Grey Hound Keepers as part of the Sultan's hunting establishment; and the 71st Cemaat Janissary Orta which had a dog tattoo, was called the Samsuncus: mastiff keepers[129]. In regards, to the Samsuncus [Saymaniyya]:

> "These Soldiers were originally the keepers of dogs used as advance forces in military campaigns. The animals would be sent in as a first strike team to maul enemies and scare them from their positions."[130]

---

126 Wittman, 1803.
127 Wittman, 1803.
128 Mikhail, 2013.
129 Nicolle, 1995.
130 Mikhail, 2013.

CHAPTER 4: ENTRENCHED BATTLE AND JANISSARY TACTICS

The Standing Army's tactics of the late 18th Century, and Napoleonic wars had changed little from the previous century[131]. Several illustrations from 1732 show large scale aerial views of the Turkish Army deployed for battle[132]. In contrast to the European Imperial Troops, who are shown arrayed in Battalions, the whole Turkish Army is shown swarming, out from its encampment in one uncoordinated mass. Other 1732 illustrations show Turkish massed behind a wall of fortified wagons, and even the whole Army forming a massed semi-circular formation.

▲ An illustration, based on 18th Century examples[133]. Typically, Janissary would collect in rough-order groupings facing their opponents.

TABUR-CENGI: DEFENSIVE FORMATION

Traditionally, Turkish were famed for their use of the Tabur-Cengi: defensive formation. Its historical origin is believed to be:

> "an effective counter to the Western Pike … [armed Soldiers] … and Musketeer formations. Tactically it was a static formation, which invited an enemy attack. From the end of the 15th Century, most European armies had adopted the use of the pike often in conjunction with firearms, forming mixed units… whereas … [Turkish] … tended to adopt purely musket and bow armed units alone supported by Artillery"[134].

The Turkish, "tactically speaking … saw musketry, supported by Light Artillery as well as bow armed troops as sufficiently capable of destroying an attack with firepower alone."[135] Traditionally fortified wagons were lined-up, and chained together, with the Artillery line creating a fixed fortified

---

131 Valentini, 1828.
132 Marsigli, 1732.
133 Marsigli, 1732.
134 Mugnai, 2015.
135 Mugnai, 2015.

palisade. At the Battle of Mohacs (29 August 1526), the Tabur-Cengi used 150 wagons and 4,000 Janissary in nine rows, with Artillery in the centre firing at close quarters[136].

> "The basic mechanism of the Tabur was simple but very difficult to apply. Before the start of the battle war wagons were chained together and cannons were placed within. Several Janissary units armed with heavy arquebuses/muskets were also positioned with the cannoneers ... [with more Janissary arranged] ... several rows deep - remained within the formation."[137]

The defensive position was occupied with several Orta armed with bows and muskets, who also helped to shield the Artillery Gunners. The rear and wings of the formation were then secured by Cavalry. By the 18th Century, Tabur-Cengi had evolved into entrenched battle formations, with an entrenched encampment at the centre of the Army deployment. At the Battle of Kartal, in 1770 the Russians reported how the Turkish Army,

> "was arrayed in a crescent, with Anatolian Cavalry on the left flank, Rumelian ... [South-Eastern European] ... Cavalry on the right, and the Tatars positioned in advance to operate as raiding parties. The Grand Vizier's huge, richly embroidered tent was pitched in the centre ... [the Janissary] ... themselves at the heart of the camp"[138].

The Turkish Army is also described using more regular deployments, as a 1770s Russian-Turkish Wars account shows:

> "immediately extended itself, and presented an uncommon spectacle. Accustomed as they were to fight in small scattered bands, the Turks now ranged themselves in European order of battle, and formed themselves in regular lines ... [Janissary] ... with the Artillery, occupying the centre, and the ... [Sipahi] ... Cavalry, taking post on the wings."[139]

ENTRENCHMENT TACTICS

Generally, on the quick march during campaigning, the common practice in European armies in the 18th Century was to bivouac, or to simply sleep in the open with the only protection being the Soldier's greatcoat. It was only during an encampment that tents were used[140]. One such bivouac is described in an account from the British campaign in Egypt – "We stuck our bayonets into the ground and slept sound ... here we made ourselves booths of the date trees, as their long branches made a good shelter from the sun and dew."[141] The common practice, in the face of the enemy was to bivouac as had been the case on the night before Waterloo, in 1815[142]. This account from the Egyptian campaign illustrates the practice of bivouac, and picketing:

> "We halted and began to dig for water, which was greatly in demand; each company dug a well and we were out of patience till the water made its appearance but before we were half satisfied the Regiment was ordered to picquet in front of the ... [French Army] ... We formed a chain of sentries"[143].

---

136 Uyar, 2009.
137 Uyar, 2009.
138 Aksan, 2002.
139 Anthing, 1813.
140 Rothenberg, 1978.
141 Low, 1911.
142 Siborne, 1848.
143 Low, 1911.

In the case of the British, in the Napoleonic period in Portugal, and Spain, Wellington, from 1810, organized tents for troops in positional areas[144][145]. It is interesting to note that in the Egyptian campaign there are frequent references to individual Regiments having their own tenting shipped by boat or camels from one night encampment to the next[146].

Traditional Janissary tactics were to set up their barracks – their tents, adjacent to the trenches they were occupying[147]. One particularly odd practice by a Janissary Orta, who likely had a pavilion-tent as its insignia, was known to have taken,

> "[a] … handful of younger Soldiers dressed as women … placed in a separate tent … called the harem … and given a special guard. They served as a sort of regimental talisman and would be defended to the death in case of defeat."[148]

A 1787 account of the Russian-Turkish War: "The Turks were no sooner disembarked, than they began to form … [entrenchments]"[149]. Turkish by the late 18th Century developed entrenchment warfare, as the basis of their Grand Army Tactics:

> "They constantly fortify their camps; and, when the day of battle arrives, draw out their forces in regular array in front of their … [entrenchments] … where their stores, tents, ammunition, and riches are deposited."[150]

It is generally known Turkish trench work was, "deeper and longer with curves rather than the standard European sharp angles … [zigzag trenches]"[151]. Whereas commonly European armies used trenches in a specific siege context, the Turkish Army were the first to entrench before the enemy in battle, as we now regularly see armies doing. A 1721 painting showing Turkish fighting the Polish Army illustrates Infantry firing from a trench dug into the ground[152]. The trench appears deep and wide enough to give cover to the chest-height allowing two ranks of Infantry to stand-up to fire their muskets. This suggests a trench approximately five feet deep, and six feet wide (1.5 by 1.8 meters). The spoil from the trench excavation has been piled behind, allowing a sconce (raised earthwork) for Artillery. The Infantry in the trench stand below the muzzles of the cannon. It is likely the Artillery was able to fire directly at any approaching enemy troops, unhampered by the Infantry Musketeers literally, under the guns, firing their own weapons. This was a variation of the famed Tabur-Cengi. Dug by the Janissary and specialist Legamdji: Miners and Sappers. It is likely that Infantry carried a substantial number of digging tools, or that a large component of a field unit was in fact dedicated diggers.

Entrenchment tactics used by Turkish appear to have involved a wide distribution of their forces. For instance, at the Battle of Forhani, in 1789 the Austrian and Russian advancing corps faced large-scale Cavalry attacks, of 15,000 and 20,000 Soldiers from the left and right flanks, which were well ahead of the Turkish Infantry entrenchments[153]. The trench line itself was weak, said to be, "ill raised, and not strengthened with sufficient Artillery"; a fact supported by the capture of only

---

144 Rothenberg, 1978.
145 Wellington, 1844.
146 Low, 1911.
147 Sakul, 2013.
148 Nicolle, 1998.
149 Anthing, 1813.
150 Alison, 1840.
151 Sakul, 2013.
152 Cavuszade, 1721.
153 Anthing, 1813.

▶ A cross-section view of a typical Turkish Infantry trench with earth bags used to build the parapet, and spare Turkish digging implement to keep enlarging and repairing the trench.

twelve pieces of cannon[154]. Trenches protected the camp, which was described as, "very rich, and … [containing] … immense magazines."[155] Russian and Austrian forces, encountered to the rear of the main Turkish entrenched camp two fortified Convents; one of these the Convent of Saint Samuel, which contained, "a considerable magazine of provisions … [was positioned] … in the rear, at a small distance from the … [entrenchments]"[156]. The other detachment was, "not far from this Convent was that of Saint John, in which also was a great magazine of provisions."[157] The Convents appear to have been each held by 200 to 300 Soldiers. Entrenchment tactics did not follow a set-piece battle layout, instead sending large tactical divisions ahead of the main entrenched Army camp. For instance, at the Battle of Heliopolis, in Egypt the Grand Vizier's Advanced Guard, comprising a force of six thousand picked Janissary established their camp well away from the main Turkish Army camp in the neighborhood of El-Hanka[158]. Janissary, it is said: "[had] … thrown up some rude fortifications", at the village of Matarieh[159]; also called, "Matharieh"[160]. This camp, "had been entrenched and armed with sixteen pieces of Artillery"[161]; and contained, "ammunition, tents"[162]. To the right of the Janissary position, there was a 1,200 Mameluke Regiment of Ibrahim-bey deployed as far as the banks of the Nile.

▲ Using woods and a river for protection, the Turkish Army has camped and entrenched. (1) The left Cavalry wing maneuvers far ahead to attack oncoming enemy troops. (2) Small units of Janissary Skirmishers occupy woods to harass oncoming enemy troops. (3) Janissary with Artillery defend a trench line. (4) Janissary sword attacks advancing enemy Infantry. (5) Cavalry reserve protects the camp and may dismount and fight alongside Janissary in the trench line. (6) Entrenched heavy cannon and Cannon Janissary. (7) The right Cavalry wing maneuvers far ahead to attack oncoming enemy troops.

---

154 Anthing, 1813.
155 Anthing, 1813.
156 Anthing, 1813.
157 Anthing, 1813.
158 Phillips, 1803.
159 Alison, 1842.
160 Phillips, 1803.
161 Phillips, 1803.
162 Alison, 1842.

PONTOON BRIDGE DEFENCES

Early exponents of pontoon bridge engineering, the Turkish fortified their camps making use of rivers and waterways to secure them. The fortified bridge-ends only appear within the camp itself, and do not appear to have been constructed at both ends, as is typically seen in a Tete de Pont. The Turkish version of these fortifications may have been intended as a last bastion for the defence of the camp, covering an escape route, from the camp in case of defeat. Allowing Soldiers to quickly destroy the pontoons stopping an attacker.

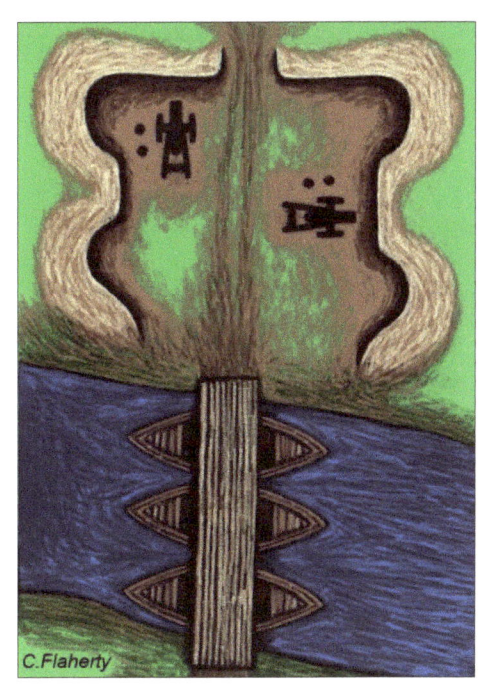

▶ An illustration of a Tete de Pont: fortified bridge-end within a Turkish camp connected to a pontoon bridge, based on 1732 example[163].

---

163 Marsigli, 1732.

JANISSARY INFANTRY TACTICS IN GENERAL

The general historical view is that, "we have very limited information about Janissary combat formations and how they actually fought"[164]. Janissary were renowned classically for their high levels of discipline, courage and training; in particular, "personal valour … had been a part of the … [Turkish] … military ethos for centuries."[165] Only a few Junior Officers were available to lead an Orta. Rather than rely on their Officers, Janissary had a much greater capacity for self-organization. Tactically speaking this had some disadvantages, as Janissary attacks frequently, "disordered … [the] … crowd of Turks … and … the attack of that of the Turks … returns to the charge as rapidly as it is dispersed."[166]

(1) Volley Fire Tactics

Janissary volley fire techniques were established by the start of the Long War, in the 1600s[167]. It is known, that Janissary used volley fire by the 1590s, and by the 16th Century Janissary fired their weapons row-by-row[168]. This tactic has also been described as meeting an enemy attack, "firing in volleys by rotating the ranks."[169] However, this general view of Janissary volley fire is somewhat contradicted, as it is stated: "[they] … never used musketry in massed volleys, relying instead on individual skills and marksmanship."[170] Eyewitness accounts from 1605, describe Janissary volley fire practice. The Orta was drawn-up in three ranks; with each Soldier ready with his match-cord lit. Most illustrations traditionally show extra lit and smoldering match cord tied loosely around the left-arm or wrist[171]. The cycle of fire (likely over a minute – as this was the typical rate of reloading time), beginning with the first rank firing their weapons[172]. The first rank bends-down to reload, while the next rank fires, and they themselves bend-down (reloading). The third rank then fires over the backs of the first two ranks that are in the process of reloading. After, the third rank has fired, the first rank stands again, and fires their weapons (with the back-third rank taking the time to reload). It has been calculated that Janissary volley fire techniques allowed a minimum delivery of nearly 330 rounds per-rank, every 20 seconds; and approximately 1,000 rounds at their target every minute (depending on the units' size). The amount of weapons fire delivered by a Janissary Musketeer Orta, and how long this fire-fight lasted is open to conjecture.

(2) Line Formations and Column Tactics

Traditionally, Janissary are known to have formed several rows deep within defensive formations. Illustrations of military formation from 1732, show Janissary adopting one of two moving columns, one is two long files spaced apart, the other is four close parallel files; and this particular formation shows each row staggered, likely to allow two or several rows to face an enemy and fire at once[173]. 16th Century Court painting often shows Janissary in line formations of two to three staggered ranks, allowing Soldiers at intervals to load, fire and reload simultaneously. Janissary and other Foot

---

164 Uyar, 2009.
165 Buyukakca, 2007.
166 Valentini, 1828.
167 Borekci, 2006.
168 Agoston, 2011.
169 Uyar, 2009.
170 Nicolle, 1995.
171 Knotel, 1890.
172 Borekci, 2006.
173 Marsigli, 1732.

Soldiers are shown, commonly in Court paintings deployed directly behind the Artillery firing over these in long lines; some of whom are deployed in long queues. This may be representing tactics involving Infantry moving in column. Another formation shown is two long single-file columns of Janissary depicted marching between cannons, for rapid deployment into a volley firing-line. Illustrations may indicate Janissary were able to undertake column advances through the spaces, where they launched offensive sorties, between the individual cannons.

This tends to suggest a high level of tactical sophistication, where Artillery fire is used to bombard the attacking force, at longer range; giving the Infantry opportunity to advance along these fire corridors. Tactics such as these maximize the effect of the cannons – keeping the advancing enemy under fire for as long as possible (tactics, such as these would come to dominate the later Napoleonic battlefield). These tactics

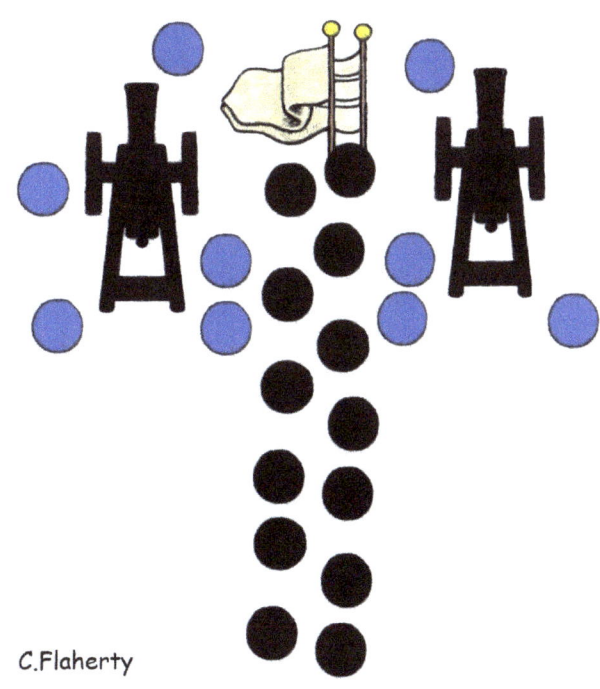

▲ **Long single-files of Janissary march between cannons, for rapid deployment into a firing-line.**

also compensated for the lack of firepower and limited range of muskets. Taking the offensive, the whole column could forge forward, in an all-out assault at full running speed when the enemy was within close-proximity, and had already lost coherent battle formation, having been continuously under fire from cannon and small arms.

▼ **By 1810, a Janissary Sub-Unit of some 30 Soldiers, like most Turkish Infantry were adopting two, or more ranks in line formation, with a Flag Bearer, and Officer leading from the center, out in front of the Soldier's block formation. It is not clear if this was a basic parade formation, or used on the battlefield.**

(3) Deep Tactical Formations

It is known, Janissary traditionally preferred deep formations deployed in several rows. The formation allowed them to achieve a continuous barrage of fire by rotating rows forward. This in fact may be referring to the column deployments between individual cannon, as these are shown to be several ranks deep in period illustrations. Janissary mainly employed deep formations only when on the defensive, such as when they were deployed between the cannons protecting them, and increasing the firepower of the whole Artillery line at close range with their musket fire as the enemy approached. The key to these formations:

> "for the Turks were cunning enough to make several false attacks, and to place considerable corps of reserve, one behind the other, which, suddenly checking the imprudent pursuit of the Christians, might drive them back, and penetrate into the openings of their lines."[174]

(4) Three-Line Infantry Formations and Skirmish Parties

The general view of Infantry tactics was that only Nizam-i Cedit: New Order Army, "training was based on French military manuals, with the Infantry drawn up in two or three lines to provide reserves and mutual support."[175] Nevertheless, an English account from Egypt, in 1800 provides a description of Janissary three-line Infantry formations and Skirmish Parties: "The Turks formed in three lines … [and] … advancing briskly on our left, their … front line formed … and discharged their muskets … [a French attack forced back the front line] … They fell back on their 2nd and 3rd lines when they all got into confusion"[176]. It is known that an Infantry attack, "advanced in groups of 40 to 50, one rank or group advancing and firing while the second reloaded, maintaining their steady advance in the face of considerable losses."[177] In the Napoleonic period, Janissary organization and tactics began to resemble the Light Infantry ethos: "Their discipline and mode of fighting was very similar to the English Light Infantry or French Tirailleurs."[178] It is known, that some Janissary were purposed in the Napoleonic period as trained Light Infantry; namely, "the 39th Orta was designated as Light Infantry and the 44th Orta is known to have been deployed in skirmish order in several battles."[179] There is an earlier account from the 1770s Russian-Turkish Wars, which identifies Janissary first, "advanced in skirmishing … [and being] … accustomed as they were to fight in small scattered bands"[180]. There is another 1770s reference to Turkish skirmish tactics, namely: "The Turkish Infantry posted themselves behind the hedges, where they did considerable mischief"[181]. There is some indication that in the 18th Century, the Janissary absorbed the Rayas: Musketeer Sharpshooter. These were a peasant class in Europe, who had become proficient huntsmen; originally recruited as auxiliaries, they were organized into companies of 50 to 100 men each. It is known that the, Rayas were rarely organized into larger units. As they were usually assigned to the Janissary for use as Skirmishers and for other traditional Light Infantry duties[182]. At the Battle of Heliopolis, in Egypt there is a report of the French during their advance being attacked by Turkish, "sharp-shooters, who were concealed in the wood."[183]

---

174 Valentini, 1828.
175 Nicolle, 1998.
176 Low, 1911.
177 Nicolle, 1998.
178 Alison, 1840.
179 Johnson, 1988.
180 Anthing, 1813.
181 Anthing, 1813.
182 Johnson, 1988.
183 Phillips, 1803.

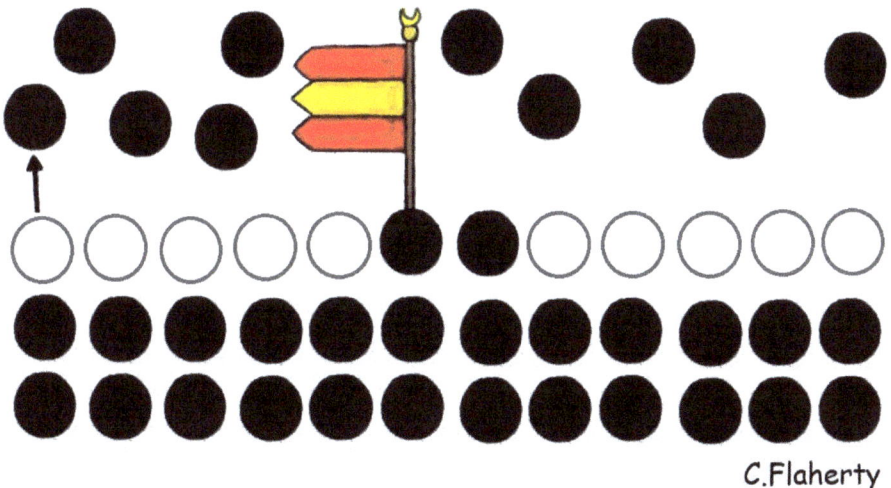

▲ The forward line of a Janissary block, upwards to a third if the force break-ranks and deploys into a mass of skirmishes.

(5) Surrounding and Round Formations

Several illustrations of military formation from 1732, show the Janissary moving in small circular groups, each led by a Flag Bearer, and these groups are clustered in a checkerboard fashion[184]. Strictly speaking, Janissary did not practice forming square against Cavalry for the Infantry. Traditionally, the Infantry was entrenched, or were given close flanking cover by the Sipahi Cavalry. Solak traditionally, when they accompanied the Sultan into the field, practiced a surrounding formation where they completely encircled the Sultan covering him from attack. This same maneuver was likely used by the personal guards. Use of spaced circular formations, appears to have led to Turkish not adopting a formal battle front:

> "The presenting of a front, or the regular deployment of troops, was as little practiced among the Turks of that period as among those of the present day: they constantly brought forward contiguous swarms, which often entirely surrounded … [their opponent] … a mode of fighting which perhaps naturally resulted from their superiority in point of numbers, and from the general ardour with which this furious multitude rushed to the attack."[185]

MASS ATTACKS WITH THE KILIJ: SCIMITAR-SWORD

The general 18th Century opinion of Janissary hand-to-hand combat abilities was: "In close or single combat, whether in the field or in the breach, the European bayonet has never proved a match for the Turkish … [scimitar]"[186]. A Turkish commentator of the period, stated:

> "[Europeans] … overpower us … by the superiority of their fire, which, in fact, it is impossible to approach; but let them leave their abominable Batteries, and encounter us like brave men hand to hand, and we shall soon see whether these infidels can resist the slaughtering sabre of the true-believers."[187][188]

---

184 Marsigli, 1732.
185 Valentini, 1828.
186 Alison, 1840.
187 Watts, 1997.
188 Aksan, 2002.

▼ The following illustration is based on originals showing Janissary moving in small circular groups, each led by a Flag Bearer[189]. These groups are clustered in a checkerboard fashion.

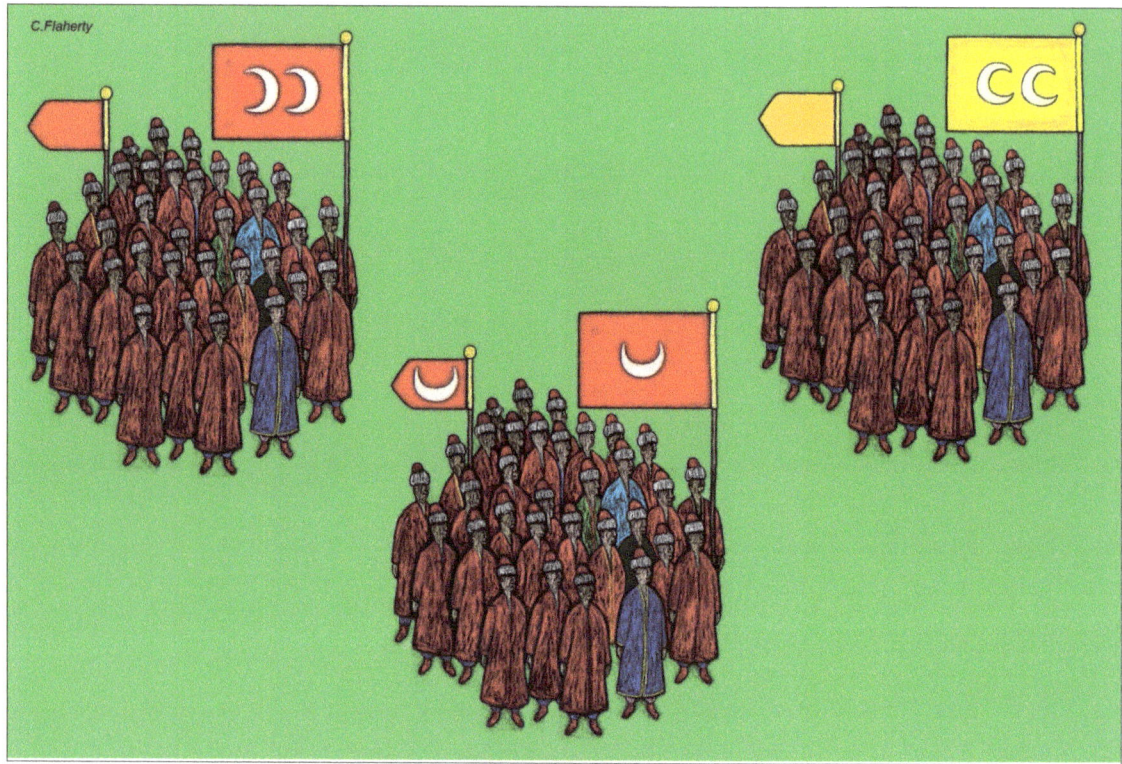

At an apt moment, the fire-fight with the enemy would cease and Janissary would charge the enemy fighting individually with their bladed personal weapons. Typically, the Janissary would attack, "in a dense mass, with swords and other weapons – usually a single rush in a wedge formation."[190] A description of Janissary massed surges, states: "boldly advanced from all quarters in close masses."[191] The attack culminating:

> "No sooner did the ... [Janissary] ... perceive that the enemy were approaching their ... [entrenchments] ... than they sallied forth with their redoubtable ... [scimitar] ... in their hands, and commenced a furious attack on the French squares."[192]

There is a 1787 Russian account, of a sword attack where it mentions, "the Turks, with their sabres and their poniards, made sad havoc among ... [the Russian Soldiers]."[193] The poniard is a small, slim dagger. There is a direct 18th Century historical parallel with Janissary massed attacks with the Kilij, and that of Highlands' charge. Both types of attacks were intended as battlefield shock tactics. Key differences can be seen, the tactic of Highlands' clans involved use of firearms during their actual charging attack, within the last 60 yards: 55 meters, relying on the smoke from the discharge of their weapons providing cover from view. Highlands' attack was highly dependent on speed and use of ground to give cover from the opposing troops' musket fire. Speed and momentum were so important to the Highlanders, that they preferred attacking downhill against an opponent. Highlanders, it

---

189 Marsigli, 1732.
190 Nicolle, 1995.
191 Valentini, 1828.
192 Alison, 1842.
193 Anthing, 1813.

is said, would discard their lower body clothing, prior to an attack to increase their speed and agility. Highlanders are known to have crouched low to the ground before making their final rush. Compared to the Highlands' clans, an account of the Janissary sword charge against a formed French line in Egypt, at the Battle of Heliopolis, appears to have been a direct dash:

> "But … valor could affect nothing against European steadiness and discipline; the … [Turkish] … were received in front by a murderous rolling fire, and charged at the same time, while disordered by their rush forward, in flank. In a few minutes they were mown down and destroyed".[194]

BATTLEFIELD HEAD-HUNTING

A 17th Century illustration depicts a Deli Cavalry Soldier holding a decapitated captive head[195]. At the 1810 Russian-Turkish Battle of Battin, it was commented, how a Russian Infantry column was destroyed entering the Turkish encampment trenches, "and the bravest of his followers who crossed it left their heads in the hands of the Turks, who fought like desperadoes."[196] Head collecting was a key aspect of Turkish military practice. In one account from the Russian-Turkish Wars,

> "the Grand Vizier wrote to the … [Sultan] … that so numerous were the heads taken off the infidel, that they would make a bridge from earth to heaven."[197]

> "It is the common custom after an action, when the Grand Vizier returns to his tent, for the Soldiers to line the path with heads which have been thus chopped off."[198]

Beheadings of the dead and wounded in battle were a common practice, and frequently occurred on a massive scale. Soldiers even carried a special weapon for the task: "Every Turk ... carries with him ... a long, and somewhat curved dagger or knife (the inward curve having the sharp edge), called a Kinschal, which he uses principally in cutting off heads."[199] At the 1811 Turkish crossing of the Danube, there was a similar account of a Russian repulse, where the Russian commander lost, "2,000 of his best troops … [when] … the Turks, with deafening shouts and sabre in hand, sallied out of their … [entrenchments] … and cut-off the heads of the slain and unfortunate wounded."[200]

A German commentator, noted somewhat disparagingly, head-hunting was mainly the actions of a bad element, "[in the Turkish] … Army … the rabble, who do nothing but plunder the dead and cut-off heads after a victory"[201]. That same commentator noted, "[in the] … field, the Grand Vizier appears as a man who has nothing else to do than to receive heads and ears"[202]. Modern historical accounts record the Turkish practice of battlefield head-hunting, and its financial incentive:

> "Chopping off the corpses heads is quite appalling for the modern observer just as much as it was for the contemporaries. One might collect the heads of the enemy corpses on the battlefield … in the

---

194 Alison, 1842.
195 Ralamb, 1658.
196 Alison, 1841.
197 Alison, 1840.
198 Eton, 1798.
199 Valentini, 1828.
200 Alison, 1841.
201 Valentini, 1828.
202 Valentini, 1828.

> hopes of material reward, as revealed in countless … [Turkish] … narrative sources."[203]

It is known, "heads of the enemy's subjects are valued by the … [Turkish] … Government at a certain price, and for every one that is brought in five sequins … [a Venetian gold coin] … are paid out of the treasury."[204] A passage from an Egyptian campaign account, describes the tent of the Turkish Grand Bashaw [Pasha]: Admiral and General in Egypt, in 1800:

> "[who] … sat in state on velvet cushions distributing rewards in money to every Turk who brought a Frenchman's head, and they were scattered through the fields in search of heads and were not very nice as to how or where they obtained them; it was said that some of our … [British] … Soldiers' heads were among them. I went to view the horrid spectacle of a pile of heads, and beheld with detestation the exulting manner in which they brought them in and the way they kicked them about"[205].

An English diplomat's account from Egypt, also pointed to a transactional and profit motive to head collecting, by Soldiers:

> "a principle of self-interest seems to pervade all ranks; and this is carried so far, that I have seen the heads of their own companions displayed before the Grand Vizier at the Battle of Heliopolis, merely to receive the reward attached to every man who brings the head of an enemy."[206]

Recorded, in an English journal of the Egyptian campaign: "Some Albanians, who pushed on, got hold of five unfortunate French Soldiers, whose heads they unmercifully cut-off, and brought back with them, to claim the reward of their barbarity; for a certain sum is, given by the Turkish Commanders for the head or ears of an enemy."[207] Napoleonic period Turkish Soldier's pay was a daily-rate of one penny and two-pence, using the British currency of the period as an example[208]; by comparison a British Soldier receive one shilling. Janissary received only a small amount of pay, even by Turkish standards: "Infantry … receive rather small pay."[209] The pay that was received, was only enough for them to buy, "bows, arrows and clean collars."[210] Extra money, such as bonuses – "were given for distinguished service, as when the survivors of the Serdengecti: Head-Risker, and Dil Kihc: Naked Sword … [Soldiers] … got extra pay"[211]. Head-hunting was therefore a lucrative business, offering financial rewards to those who could collect heads. An account of the Turkish Governor of Acre during Napoleon's siege, during the major French assaults against his palace citadel, described how, "Djezzar … [Governor] … was sitting in a conspicuous place, surrounded by the mutilated members of the assailants, and by turns rewarding such as brought him heads and distributing … [musket] … cartridges, they were busily employed in preserving his residence and himself from destruction."[212] The practice of paying for heads, continued up to the Sultan:

> "They cut-off the heads of the dead as well as of the living, and collect them in the same manner as the heads, claws, or snouts of noxious wild beasts are delivered to the authorities appointed to reward the slayers. The custom, which has been questioned by modern historians, of collecting the noses

---

203 Sakul, 2012.
204 Eton, 1798.
205 Low, 1911.
206 Morier, 1801.
207 Walsh, 1803.
208 Morier, 1801.
209 Dalvimart, 1802.
210 Nicolle, 1995.
211 Nicolle, 1995.
212 Camden, 1814.

and tips of the ears of their enemies, is literally true. When, after a successful affair, the quantity of heads becomes too considerable for conveyance, those smaller salted parts are forwarded in sacks, as testimonials of their good fortune. The ... [Sultan] ... awards payment for these trophies of extirpation, but prefers receiving entire heads, in order that they may be fixed on poles in the capital, with all suitable ... [brilliant display]."[213]

In general, it appears that Turkish would opportunistically collect heads anytime during a battle: "All those who had been killed or wounded had their heads cut-off by the Turks and Arabs."[214] An English account from Napoleon's siege of Acre, which involved a combined British and Turkish sally-attack on the French besieging entrenchments during which they were compelled to retreat; it was complained: "the ... [Turkish] ... agreeably to the usual barbarity of their practice, were more active in collecting heads, than in endeavoring to annoy their opponents."[215] A similar incident is recorded during the Battle of Aboukir where General Bonaparte saw an opportunity to finally breakthrough the Turkish camp entrenchments. Said to have seen large numbers of Soldiers leave their trenches to collect prize-heads, whereupon he launched a successful counterattack finally breaking into the Turkish camp having caught the defenders completely disorganized as they were too preoccupied collecting heads[216].

European commentators saw head-hunting as, "barbarous usages of the Turks"[217]; but not militarily effective, and somewhat typical of the 18th Century mindset,

> "The Prince de Ligne observed, on this practice of the Turks, to cut-off the heads of the wounded or prisoners, that it was more formidable in appearance than reality; for it could do no harm to the dead, it was often a relief to the wounded, and that it was rather an advantage to the unhurt, as it left them no chance of escape but in victory."[218][219]

Commentators in the 18th Century, were highly critical of atrocities committed by Turkish troops, such as the wanton killing and decapitation of prisoners[220]. Turkish Soldiers were also known to accept foreign Soldiers' surrender, such as that of the French Garrison of the Ionian Islands, and along the Dalmatian coast, in 1799. French prisoners of war, repatriated by 1802, were treated no differently to any other European prisoner of war in the Napoleonic period. Instances where Turkish decapitated dead prisoners are known – the explanation, this act was not for any financial motivation, or even as an act of barbarity, but rather as a bureaucratic action, "to prove that the captive neither ran away nor suffered an unauthorized execution during the march."[221] This act of accounting for heads, may have been common practice, as one early Napoleonic account mentions a specific number of heads being presented to the Grand Vizier, who, "had upwards of forty heads brought to him on the field of battle."[222] All these heads were paid for by the Grand Vizier himself, and he was ultimately paid by the Sultan, when these heads were bagged and sent to Constantinople as part of the reporting on the progress of the Army in the war.

---

213 Valentini, 1828.
214 Walsh, 1803.
215 Camden, 1814.
216 Scott, 1827.
217 Valentini, 1828.
218 Valentini, 1828.
219 Alison, 1841.
220 Eton, 1798.
221 Sakul, 2012.
222 Wittman, 1803.

CHAPTER 5: TRADITIONAL ARTILLERY

The traditional Turkish Artillery used field cannon like Darbzen, Kolunburna and Sahi in line positions, or in trench lines. There were also Guns of Position like the Balyemez and stone firing cannons.

DARBZEN

It is known, some three hundred Darbzen were cast for the 1596 Hungarian campaign. Darbzen fired a 1.5-Okka (a Turkish mass of weight approximately 1.29 kilograms) ball weight; or 1.2 to 2.5 kilograms ball (the equivalent of a 5½-pounder gun). A 1732 illustration depicts a swivel gun, with a Gunner and transport camel[223]. Larger Darbzen had a crew of three[224], possibly mounted on a light field carriage, or some kind of frame. At the Battle of the Pyramids, at Embabeh, in 1798, deployed along the Janissary and Musketeers entrenched firing-line, some 40 in number, "guns, wanting carriages, were mounted on clumsy wooden frames."[225] Darbzen could have been mounted on a type of tripod-triangular timber frame, based on the tetrahedron: triangular pyramid wood tower frame featured in the 74th Cemaat Janissary Orta badge[226].

▶ An illustration from 1732, shows a Darbzen swivel cannon suspended from the side of a camel with its rider, identified as the, "Canonier Turc."[227] Depicted holding a lit fuse this has often been interpreted, as somehow firing the cannon from the camel's sides. A rope tied around the cannon button is depicted controlling elevation.

KOLUNBURNA

18th Century Kolunburna: field cannon design and designation had remained unchanged from earlier periods. Generally, these were single piece cast bronze cannons. Firing stone or cast-iron projectiles. Cannons ranged according to 8- to 22-Okka calibre guns, which fired a 10 to 27 kilograms ball (making the later equivalent of a 59½-pounder cannon). Field mobile Kolunburna (similar to

---

223 Marsigli, 1732.
224 Agoston, 2005.
225 Scott, 1827.
226 Sevket, 1907.
227 Marsigli, 1732.

European Culverins), were used as lighter field guns, and ranged between 1.5- to 7-Okka calibre guns, which fired a 1 to 9 kilograms ball (making the later equivalent of a 19½-pounder cannon). A 1798 illustration of a, "ancien canon de campagne": old field cannon depicts a barrel approximately 8 feet long[228]. Illustrations from 1805, and 1813, show heavier Turkish field cannon with a field carriage, with its front-ends of the sides reinforced with covering iron plates secured with a double row of bolts[229][230]. Painted dark red-brown, the carriage sides are reinforced with metal edging, and the spoked wheels have reinforcing iron tire brackets. Another 1798 illustration depicts, "[a] … newly invented large cannon", with a highly decorated barrel and fish handles, which was approximately 9 feet long[231]. The carriage was similar to standard late-18th Century European heavy cannon field carriages with Turkish solid wheel types.

▼ **Darbzen swivel cannon transport camel with its Cannoneer Rider. The 1732 illustration depicts a cannon fired from the camel's sides. The cannon was too large to be used like saddle mounted Zamburechki, or Musquetooners (large-bore cannon-muskets), in common use at the time in Persian, Turkish and Egyptian armies by Arab Tribal Cavalry. More strapping has been added to secure the cannon hanging on the side than originally depicted. A rug-woven caparison covers the cannel's back. Rather than another cannon carried on the opposite side, a large camel saddle carry bag – this is a later 19th Century Turkish Army example, filled with tools and shot could have been used.**

---

228 Raif, 1798.
229 Unknown, 1805.
230 Kobell, 1813.
231 Raif, 1798.

▼ A possible reconstruction of a 1732 Darbzen mounted on a frame-mount, stabilized by earth bags, and roped cannon button to control elevation, with a Gunner-Camel Transport Rider. Darbzen or Swivel Cannon could have been mounted on wagons, or spiked onto logs along a Janissary firing line. The side view of the 1732 Darbzen shows an unusual feature, as its barrel trunnions are placed low, in line with the base, rather than the usual mid-point.

SAHI

Sahi cannon types included a light gun firing shot ranging between 150 grams, to 1.8 kilograms, and some larger rounds: 4 and 6 kilograms: 3- and 5-Okka respectively; light 2- to 13-pounder cannon. The most distinctive feature was a long barrel[232]. It is known, from 1782 till 1789, Sahi carriages were identical to that used by the 1774 Sur'atcis: Speed Manoeuvre Artillery Corps[233].

▼ A 1798 illustration newly invented large cannon with a highly decorated barrel and fish handles.

---

232 Agoston, 2005.
233 Sakul, 2011.

▼ A Turkish medium to heavy field cannon around 1805, till 1813, along with a barrel for an old field cannon illustrated in 1798.

BALYEMEZ

Traditionally, Balyemez cannon were the, "largest piece in the … arsenal … [and] … was hauled overland by twenty pairs of buffalo"[234]. A 1798 Turkish description and drawing of an, "old Balyemez or cannon de batterie"[235], meaning a Gun of Position, depicts a cannon barrel: "about 3.5 … [meters] … long and judging from the approximate diameter of the cannon ball this large piece must have fired shots of some 27-35 kilograms in weight."[236][237] This would be the equivalent of a 59½ to 77-pounder cannon. It is also known the 25-Okka (70-pounder) or greater were used in sieges[238]. The immense weight of the Balyemez barrel was the likely reason for a distinctive feature of the carriage, namely use of solid wheels, seen in a 1732 illustration[239]. The 1732 Balyemez barrel was likely as long as the 1798 version, and it used a heavy single block trail carriage with heavy bolted iron bands for added strength[240]. The cannon used a solid convex shaped wheel, made of several pieces and strengthened with large iron cross braces, coming to almost 1 foot: 30 centimeters thick at the center. The wheel diameter was likely around $3^{1}/_{5}$ feet: 97 centimeters. A 1732 illustration also depicts a solid barrel wheel, and the commentary states:

> "[I] … asked them why they make such wheels, they replied that it was in order to avoid having to raise the Batteries high. In fact, this use would not harm us in places."[241]

The barrel wheel could also be used for transport over soft surfaces, relying on the wide surface area to displace the weight of the gun. This would have required a modified long iron axel.

---

234 Fleet, 2006.
235 Agoston, 2005.
236 Raif, 1798.
237 Agoston, 2005.
238 Nolan, 2008.
239 Marsigli, 1732.
240 Marsigli, 1732.
241 Marsigli, 1732.

LIGHTER GUNS OF POSITION (FORTRESS CARRIAGE CANNON)

Cannon with a heavy single block trail, not unlike the 1732 Balyemez, with heavily reinforced end-trail running wheels, is shown from the rear view[242][243], and in an 1806 illustration of a Turkish camp scene, from its side[244]. Both illustrations depict an iron winch chain, with a large hook, attached to a ring at the end of the trail. The main discrepancy is the overall size of the cannon and its carriage, as the 1806 illustration shows a larger version in relation to people standing around it. Cannon balls shown scattered on the ground appear to be for a 24-pounder (with a diameter of 5½ inches), or possibly stone versions as the barrel is shown as heavy and more strait sided with little tapering. Depicted parked in camps, has been assumed to be some type of Field Artillery[245]. However, carriages with rear running wheels are more typical of Fortress Artillery, as the small wheels are designed to run along a track controlling the guns' recoil. Possibly used as a Positional Gun, with specially set up platforms and tracks for the rear running wheels and winches set up to pull the cannons back.

▼ 1806 Fortress carriage cannon used in field fortifications as a Positional Gun.

▶ A 1732 Balyemez showing axel and barrel wheels designed for fortifications use. A top-view of the solid round wheel is shown along with the rest of the single trail carriage. The cannon displays the Tugra: insignia of Sultan Mahmud I, ruling between 1730 and 1754.

---

242 Unknown, 1817.
243 McLean, 1818.
244 Watts, 1806.
245 Johnson, 1988.

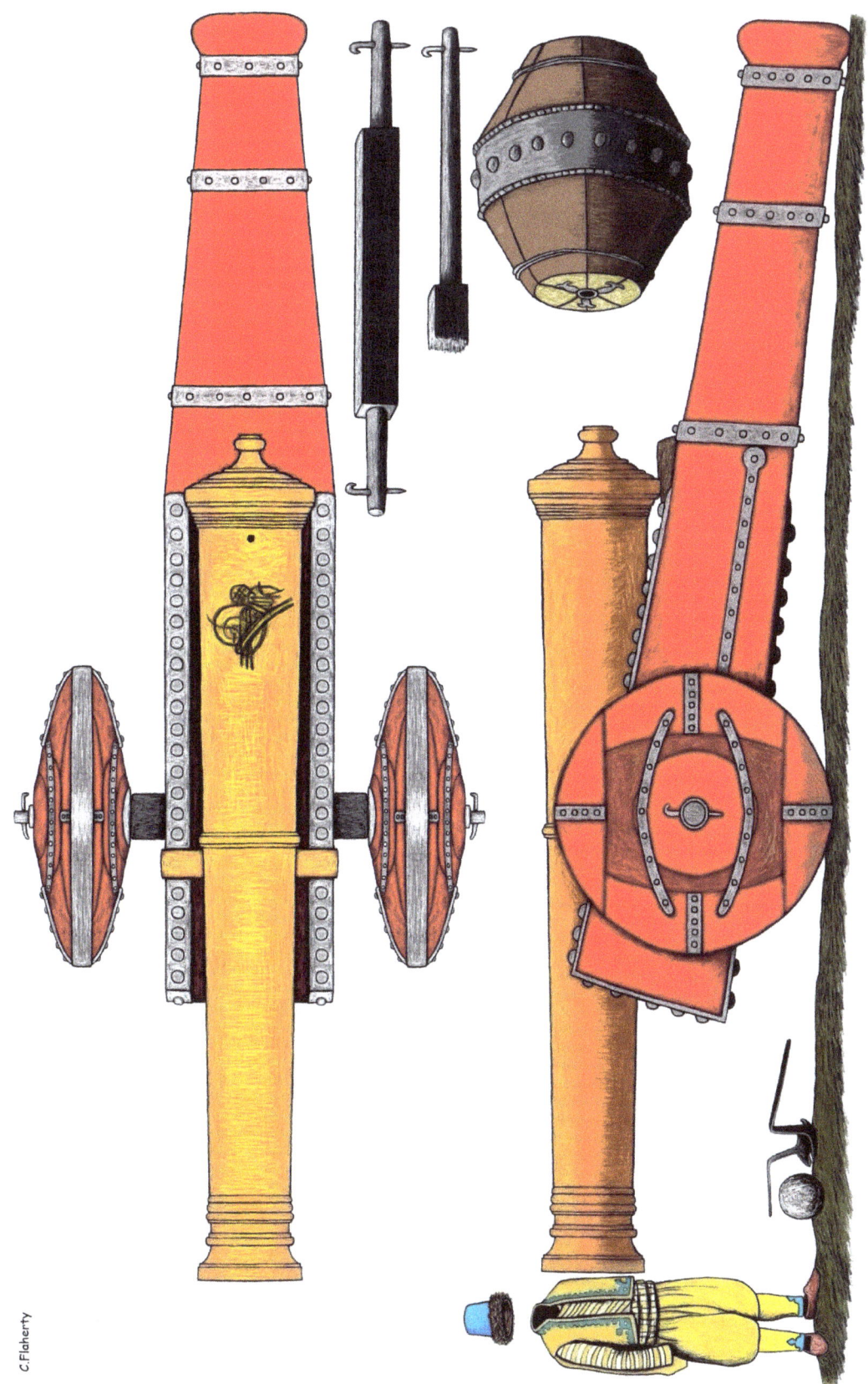

KANTAR

Stone firing cannon were operated by the Turkish in the late 18th Century, and Napoleonic period, and were ship's batteries[246]. Kantar was related to older Basilisks: Great Turkish Bombard, commonly called 'Dardanelles guns'; "and like their predecessors threw marble cannonballs."[247] The main design difference was Basilisks had long barrels, whereas Kantar, "were by contrast very short and consequently useless in anything but point blank range."[248] Kantar used less gun powered to fire, so the walls of the gun were quite thin. Kantar fire-rates was quite slow:

Range:	Some estimates suggest 1,600 meters; however, more likely only close range.
Crew:	10+
Fire rate:	15 shots per day (due to barrel overheating).

Admiral Sir John Duckworth captured stone firing cannons from the island of Kinaliada, in the Sea of Marmara, near Constantinople, in 1807. The cannons may have been part of the Turkish redoubt on the Point Pesquies destroyed during a raid that, "set fire to the gabions, and spiked the guns; eight of which were brass, and carried immensely large marble balls."[249] Kantar fired a stone shot weighing 56 kilos (approximately 125 pounds); which would have classed this gun as a, "One-Kantar", whereas a Three-Kantar fired a 336-pound shot[250].

▼ Kantar: stone firing cannon (1790 till 1810), on an Ottoman 'old or national' carriage.

---

246 Yener, 2016.
247 Yener, 2016.
248 Yener, 2016.
249 James, 1826.
250 Yener, 2016.

Duckworth's captured Kantar weighs 5.2 tonne, and was cast in 1790, or 1791 for Sultan Selim III. In Greenwich, London, the cannon sits on a cast-iron display carriage, that was made by the Royal Carriage Department, Royal Arsenal Woolwich. The original gun carriage design was either a Turkish copy of the Vauban fortress gun carriage, or more likely the Ottoman four wheeled, "old or national design", more commonly seen in the early Napoleonic period[251]. To lift these large cannon balls a variety of carriers were used. A two person lift cradle version to pick the ball up, or a cradle that could be hoisted-up with a block and tackle. On ships and in forts the block and tackle were suspended from the deck roof, or a swing crane, to haul the ball up to the gun muzzle in a net[252]. Once the cannonball was lifted to the correct height of the muzzle it was pushed-in, and rammed-home by the gun team.

▶ Cannon with end trail running wheels, and winch chain attached, or the hoist used for loading heavy stone balls into the Kantar would have required a horizontal capstan-winch, such as this 18th Century design commonly used in construction work[253].

ARTILLERY TRANSPORT

Traditionally, the cannon wagon, as it was known, was a large four-wheeled wagon with box sides operated by Arabaci: Wagoners. In addition to pulling a cannon, the wagon carried weapons, and ammunition for the cannon it towed, and for the Artillery Janissary who traditionally fought from the cannon line protecting it. Traditionally, large four-wheeled Arabaci wagon carried all the Artillery ammunition needed for a battle. The load for each cannon on campaign was typically 100 balls and gunpowder charges per battle.

ARTILLERY DRIVERS (POSSIBLE CANNONEER) UNIFORMS

A 1732 illustration of a Darbzen swivel cannon transport camel with its Cannoneer rider, identified as the, "Canonier Turc"[254], shows wearing a flat-topped conical hat, and turban, with a buttoned collarless coat with knee-length skirt and narrow sleeves, a waist sash, knee-length bloomer-pants, stockings and Turkish slipper shoes complete the dress. An 1805 group of Artillery Drivers, and possible Cannoneers appearing in an illustration of, "Turkisch Kaiserliche Artillerie": Turkish Emperors' Artillery[255]; the same group also appears in an 1813 illustration of, "Turkish Infantry"[256]. The group of Soldiers, shows one wearing a large white turban, with a white collarless knee-length shirt with narrow sleeves, and black Turkish riding boots. The next Soldier in the group, is shown from the back only, wears a red conical hat with a white turban, and long loose coat with short open sleeves over another shirt with narrow sleeves. A blue waist sash is worn over the long coat, and black Turkish riding boots complete the dress. The third in the group wears a red turban, and blue collarless vest with yellow tape edging, over a yellow (orange) shirt with lose open sleeves, and possibly a hood. Blue Russian pants, with ankle cuffs, and red Turkish slipper shoes complete the dress.

---

251 Yildiz, 2013.
252 Yener, 2016.
253 Diderot, 1772.
254 Marsigli, 1732.
255 Unknown, 1805.
256 Kobell, 1813.

CHAPTER 6: ARTILLERY UNIFORMS

Traditionally, Topchees [Topijis]: Artillery organization consisted of the following units:

| Cemaat: Artillery Regiment | 100 to 250 Gunners |
| Boluk: Artillery Files (Sub-Regiments) | 100 Gunners |

Like Janissary, Topchees Regiments each had their own Kazan[257]. Artillery Regiment's Kazan was set up in similar fashion to Janissary, in front of the Artillery tents, and played a similar role. The Topchees flag, from the late-18th Century, was a small red banner with a pointed tail, and had a wide yellow boarder[258]. The red field displayed a yellow cannon barrel and four cannon balls. The banner was carried on a yellow staff, with a spear point finial.

TOPCHEES UNIFORMS

A 1907 illustration of a Koumbaradji (Bombardier)[259], shows a low conical blue Fez hat with brown fur trim, identical to the Legamdji (which is red bodied). The uniform consists of a yellow collarless open jacket with hanging sleeves and decorative blue tape edging, worn over a yellow and white striped wrap-around shirt with narrow sleeves. A yellow and white striped waist sash is worn over yellow Russian pants, and yellow leggings with decorated blue tape edging and knot. Red Turkish slipper shoes complete the dress. The depiction matches another 1907 illustration of a, "Bonbardie"[260], that shows a near identical uniform, except the Soldier wears a Tarturas hat: a tall black stovepipe hat, and the tape edging and knot on the yellow leggings are red. An 1822 portrait of a, "le Koumbaradji: Bombardier"[261], shows this was worn by the Humbaraci: mortar troops.

An 1817 dated illustration of a, "Soldier of Turkish Artillery"[262], shows wearing a red bonnet with a blue top tassel, and large yellow and white striped turban, over a green wrap-around shirt under an open red short jacket with narrow sleeves, and some black cord-embroidered patterns on the chest and corners. A red waist sash, dark-green Russian pants and red Turkish riding boots complete the dress. Another depiction of the same Soldier without the overcoat[263][264], which appears more like a cloak, shows this as blue with four pairs of white tassel-ended chest cords.

ARTILLERY JANISSARY

Turkish Infantry fighting from cannon lines was well established in the 16th Century and often illustrated[265]. The 18th Cemaat Janissary Orta, had a three crossed-cannons tattoo badge, while the 16th Cemaat Janissary Orta with crossed cannons, and possible two flags tattoos, were traditionally known to have, "marched with the Artillery"[266].

---

257 Raif, 1798.
258 Sevket, 1907.
259 Sevket, 1907.
260 Sevket, 1907.
261 Choiseul-Gouffier, 1822.
262 Unknown, 1817.
263 Unknown, 1817.
264 McLean, 1818/
265 Topkapi, 1526.
266 Johnson, 1988.

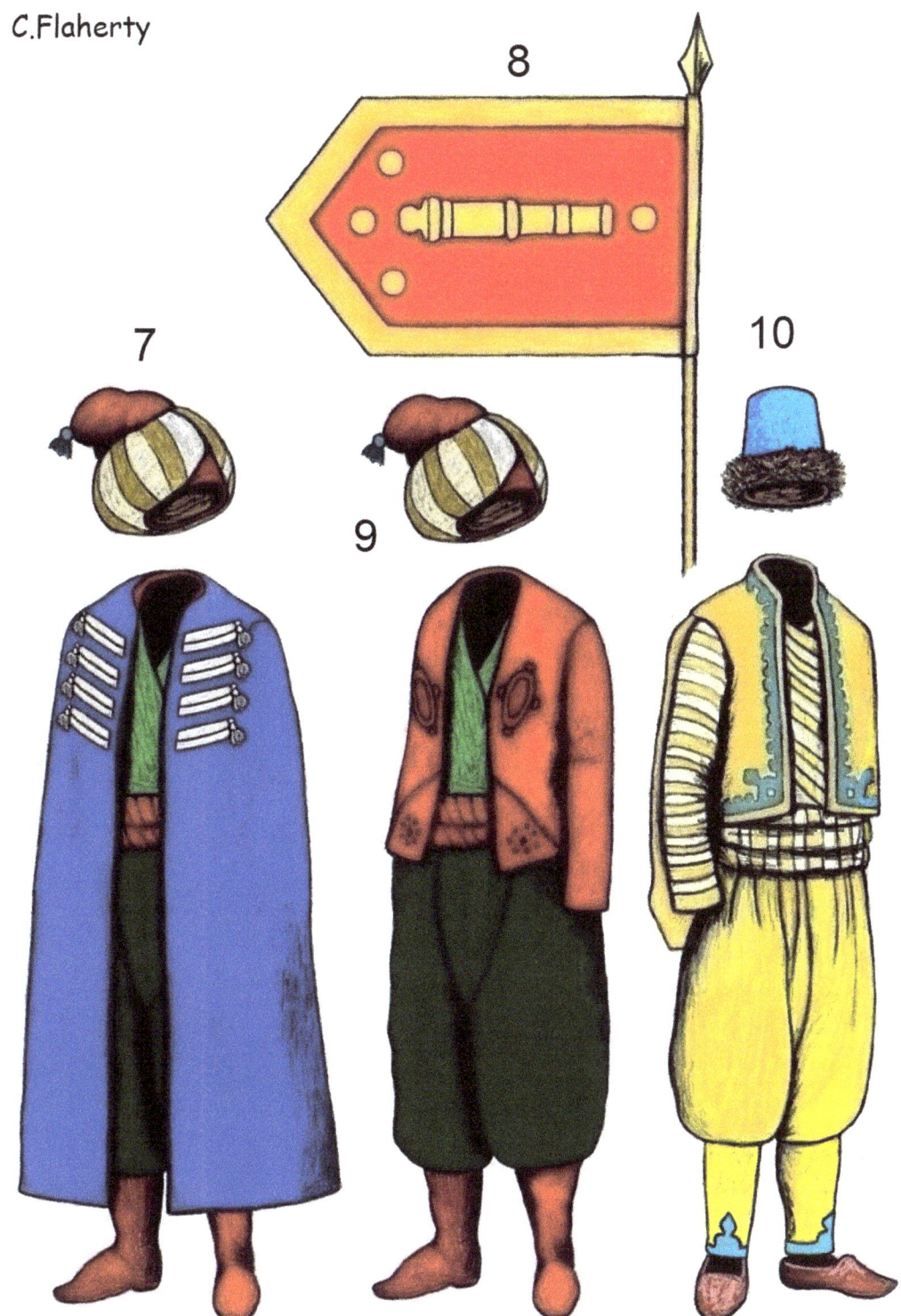

FIGURE 7: Artillery Soldier with cloak.
FIGURE 8: Topchees flag.
FIGURE 9: Artillery Soldier.
FIGURE 10: Koumbaradji: Bombardier (1750 onwards).

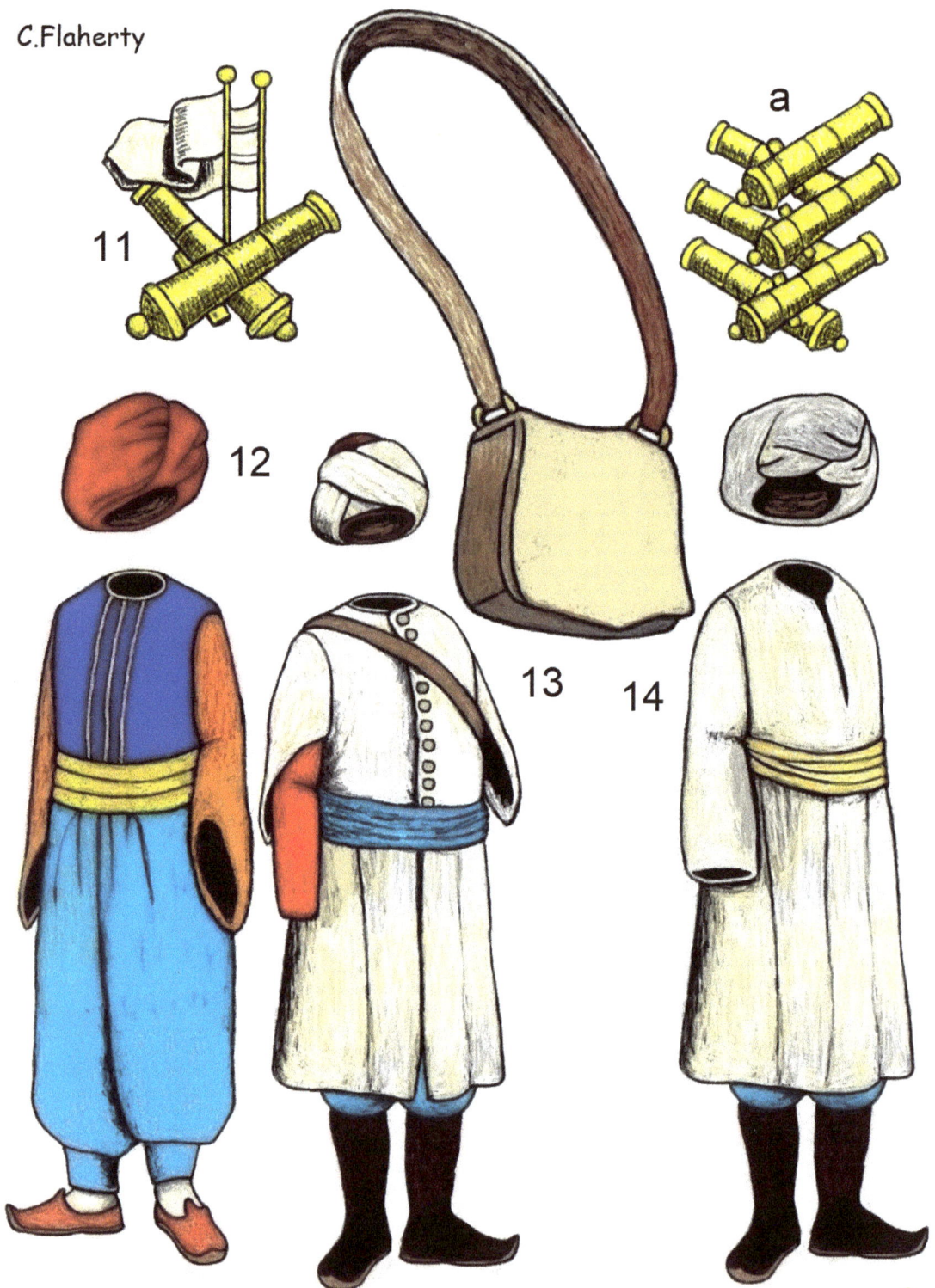

FIGURE 11: 16th Cemaat Janissary Orta tattoo; (a) 18th Cemaat Janissary Orta tattoo.
FIGURE 12: Artillery Soldier.
FIGURE 13: Artillery Soldier, with large ammunition box on carry strap details.
FIGURE 14: Artillery Soldier-Driver.

CHAPTER 7: ARTILLERY TACTICS

The Grand Vizier's Army, in Egypt, in 1800 had a small Light Artillery Column of 19 cannon and howitzers[267]. Many accounts suggest Artillery fire could be quite ineffective, such as at the Battle of Heliopolis, in 1800, where the Turkish Artillery till it was captured[268], performed poorly: "The cannonade ... balls ... ill directed, flew over the heads of the ... [French] ... while ... [the Turkish] ... Artillery was rapidly dismounted by the well-directed fire of their adversaries"[269]. It is not known if these cannon were brigaded into a large battery, or were distributed along the trench line among the Infantry. Notwithstanding poor performance in Egypt, a European commentator, generally noted that in terms of the Russian and Turkish wars over the 18th and early 19th Centuries:

> "Turkish Artillery was long superior to that of the European powers; and although it had not kept pace with the progress of Western science, and had sunk from its former celebrity during the wars of the Eighteenth Century, yet it was still formidable from the great number of guns which their armies brought into battle, and the rapidity with which their admirable horses moved them from one part of the field to another"[270].

GUNS OF POSITION BATTERY

The general practice was for the Turkish, "[to commence their] ... attack with a discharge of Artillery"[271]. Generally, Turkish Army Artillery tactics show a Battery of nine or more field cannon deployed within a single large Brigade forming a Positional Battery[272]. Guns of Position Battery is an older military term describing a specific role for heavy fieldpieces, not designed for quick movements. The concept arose during the 17th Century, with the practice of Generals dragging a collection of various cannon into battle to serve as the Guns of Position for, "preliminary bombardment of the opposing Army"[273]. Guns of Position as a military concept emerged in the English Civil War period (1642 till 1651), referring to heavy cannon placed in static positions on a battlefield[274]. Under Louis XIV (1643 till 1715), use of the heavy Guns of Position was established as a common tactical practice, placing these within protective field fortifications. In 1759, Frederick the Great, established heavier Guns of Position which were dragged by horses in single file, led by civilian drivers on foot, and were generally formed in four masses, in the centre, wings, and reserve[275]. An English account from Egypt describes a Turkish Positional Battery of heavy guns, however it might have been a locally sourced odd collection of old ordnance, as it was described: "The Turks ... brought up some clumsy pieces of Artillery"[276]. From a European perspective Turkish heavy guns would have been indistinguishable from cannon more seen as part of the 'Battering Train'. By the time of the Allied investment of Cairo and Giza, in 1801, the Turkish Army had acquired more Artillery, consisting of, "about one thousand ... [Artillery Soldiers] ... with a large Battering Train, and forty pieces of Light Artillery."[277] There is some question as to the origin of the Turkish Battering Train, as one

---

267 Morier, 1801.
268 Morier, 1801.
269 Alison, 1842.
270 Alison, 1840.
271 Anthing, 1813.
272 Topkapi, 1609.
273 Dastrup, 1992.
274 Henry, 2005.
275 Hubert, 1911.
276 Low, 1911.
277 Wittman, 1803.

Napoleonic account states how the, "Turks ... [were] ... hardly provided with any Battering Train"[278]; and, "the Turks had not been able to bring a Siege Train across the desert."[279] It is known, British on arrival in Egypt found their, "Battering Train of heavy siege-guns ... were awkward to transport overland"[280]. The solution was conversion of Royal Navy carronades fitted to carriages for land use. British converted ships' cannon was likely provided to the Turkish Army.

CANNON LINES

Paintings and illustrations show only a few individuals working a large line of guns, rather than more familiar crews of four, or five Gunners, or more working a gun each. The explanation for this lack of Gunners is they tended to shelter directly behind the guns, as these were fired by an individual Gunner in quick succession[281]. This would lead to a situation where all the guns in the line, were reloaded at once, and pushed back into line, to compensate for the inevitable recoil of the weapons themselves, which may have been reduced due to the Turkish practice of linking a heavy chain from one axel-hub hook to the next, creating a barrier with the cannons.

▼ Traditional Turkish Artillery line tactics. Artillery was either massed in a line, with troops behind, and on the flanks, waiting to advance, or placed on higher ground, or a built-up platform, with a trench at the front.

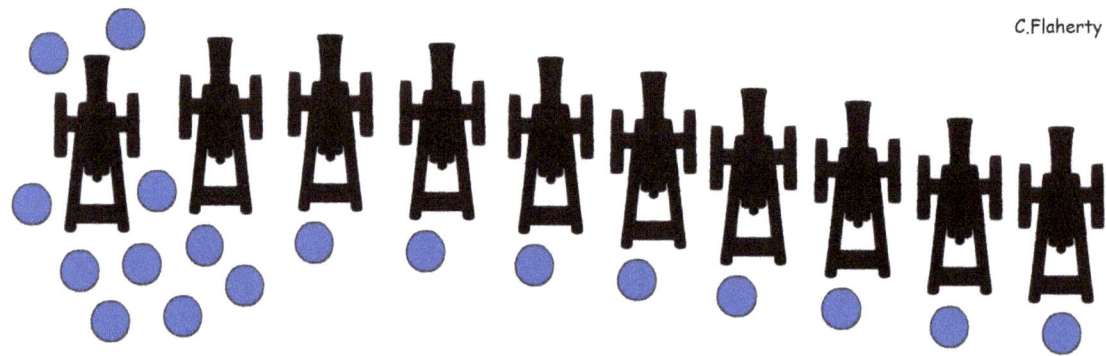

▼ In later periods, cannons were interspaced with howitzers on beds or smaller ship's carriages. A line of Infantry forms a firing line in a trench under the cannon muzzles so both forces can fire simultaneously at an oncoming opponent. A similar trench feature would have been seen in standard European cannon defensive works, the spoil from creating a ditch was piled into gabions. However, European Infantry were rarely placed in the frontal ditch. The Turkish also made extensive use of gabions in their defensive works.

---

278 Alison, 1841.
279 Mackesy, 2013.
280 Mackesy, 2013.
281 Topkapi, 1609.

A 1721 painting showing a Turkish Army fighting the Polish illustrates the Artillery component of the Standing Army transitioning from a line of several medium to heavy cannons, to a mixed battery of medium to heavy cannons and mortars on ship's carriages, placed between every three to four cannons[282].

▼ A typical heavy mortar mounted on a mobile four-wheeled ship's carriage. A 1732 illustration of the heavier Turkish stone firing bombard-mortar[283]. It rests on a heavy sled-carriage.

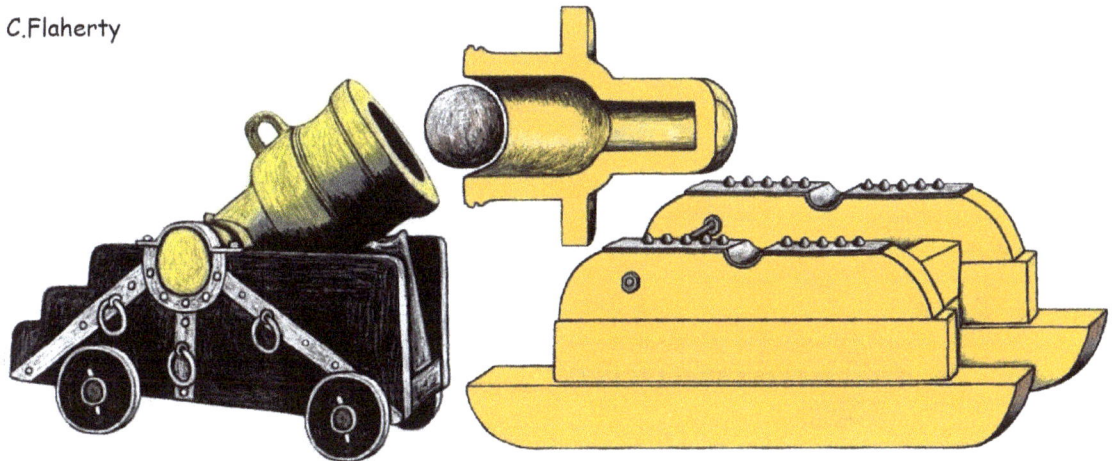

DARBZEN AND INFANTRY TRENCH LINES

Darbzen would be deployed along the Janissary firing-line, supporting the Musketeers. Use of a large number of Darbzen at the Battle of the Pyramids, at Embabeh, in 1798, it appears these guns were in concealed positions likely covered with screens, as one account states: "Mameluke … unmasked forty pieces of indifferent artillery, which they discharged upon them; but the … [French] … Divisions rushed forward with such impetuosity, that the Mameluke … had not time to re-load their guns."[284]

▲ Artillery Janissary from the 16th Cemaat Janissary Orta mix with Gunners forming a mixed Infantry and cannon line. This same cannon and Musketeers mix was used with Darbzen, and would be deployed along the Janissary firing-line, supporting the Musketeers.

282 Cavuszade, 1721.
283 Marsigli, 1732.
284 Kelly, 1831.

MOVING INFANTRY AND ARTILLERY ATTACKS

A 1788 illustration of the Turkish Army arriving at Sophia, Bulgaria, shows a maneuver, where ahead of each Infantry column a cannon is being handled forward[285]. According, to an account from Egypt in 1800, Turkish practiced moving Infantry and Artillery attacks:

> "Infantry and Artillery were drawn up in three bodies, that is, a main body and two wings, nearly in a line, with the guns in front. While the whole advanced slowly, a firing was kept up exclusively by the Artillery; and the movement having been continued for the space of six or seven hundred yards ... During the whole of the time the Infantry remained with their arms shouldered"[286].

▼ Turkish Infantry in a loosely formed column, and with its Gunners pull-push a cannon ahead ready to fire. Advancing and firing cannon line, with Infantry formed behind in a line formation.

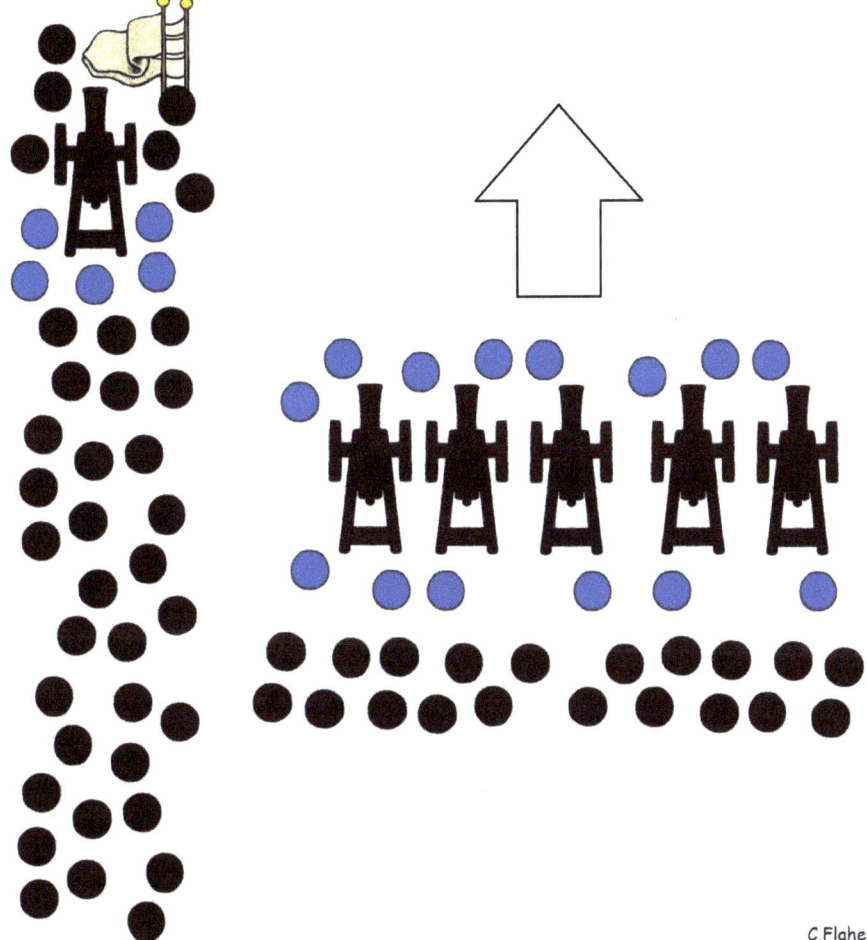

◄ Another view of the Infantry firing trench placed before the cannon at ground level or potentially placed on a sconce: raised earthwork for Artillery. The sconce is possibly only 3 feet: 1 meter high, allowing cannons to fire-overhead, and Infantry in the trench to directly fire at approaching enemy troops. This suggests a trench approximately 5 feet: 1.5 meters deep, and 6 feet: 1.8 meters wide. Spoil from trench excavations could be piled behind creating the sconce, or piled in front creating a parapet, or placed in earth bags to reinforce the parapet.

---

285 Hochenleitter, 1788.
286 Wittman, 1803.

CHAPTER 8: LEGAMDJI, CEBECI AND ARABACI

Turkish field engineering traditionally relied on the Legamdji [Lagimci Ocagi]: Hearth of Miners and Sappers, who undertook field works, fortifications and siege operations. Legamdji received specialized instruction in schools specifically set up for this purpose[287]. In Egypt, in 1800, it was noted by an English observer that among the principal officers under the command of the Grand Vizier, was the Lakemgis Bashi: Commandant of Miners[288]. In addition to the Legamdji, other sources of the skills needed for construction, came from traditional trades and craftsmen such as wood carvers, who by the 18th Century occupied a permanent position in the Army and most claimed to be Janissary[289]. Traditionally, it is known that the Janissary worked on building sites as part of their training making them, "effective Sappers on campaign."[290]

Baltadji [Baltadjis; Baltaci]: Axeman, woodcutter, pioneer, or halberdier, were said to have been recruited from the Janissary Djivelek: Juvenile Soldiers[291]. Axemen were traditionally used to remove obstacles from the path of the Army: clearing trees, levelling roads, and filling swamps. Axemen also gave its name to a special Guard Company in the Sultan's palace: "[They] … were a sort of lictors who headed the procession when the Sultan appeared in state"[292]. It is known that the Court Axemen were enrolled in the Sultan's Household Guard Kapikulu Sipahi and Silahtar Cavalry Regiments.

An illustration of a Legamdji[293], shows a low conical red Fez hat with fur trim, identical to the Artillery Soldiers (which was blue bodied). The Legamdji is shown wearing a white wrap-around shirt, with rolled-up sleeves, with a possible undershirt. Light-blue knee-length bloomer-pants, bare legs and red Turkish slipper shoes complete the dress.

▶ Legamdji (1750 onwards), with 17th Century axe, pick and earth bags commonly used in engineering and fortification works, along with a Turkish spade.

---

287 Sakul, 2013.
288 Wittman, 1803.
289 Nicolle, 1995.
290 Nicolle, 1995.
291 Brill, 1913.
292 Blackwood, 1841.
293 Sevket, 1907.

Legamdji used typical 16th and 17th century European mining tools. It should be noted, that the Legamdji were traditionally seen as superior skilled compared to their European rivals, especially regarding construction of narrow galleries, with lower ceilings, to increase the force of a mine blast. This was due to the fact they, "used to dig in a sitting position"[294]. Commonly seen in miniature paintings from the classical period was the Turkish triangle-shaped spade with a long iron back-bar.

CEBECI

Cebeci [Cebeci Ocagi]: Hearth of Armourers role was to maintain and transport Janissary weapons, armour, and ammunition. Traditionally, Cebeci used four-wheeled cannon transport wagons[295]. An early illustration of a Cebeci shows an Armoured Infantry Soldier[296]. Cebeci was one of the privileged units numbering no more than 625 Soldiers in 1574. During peacetime Cebeci kept all weaponry in the Cephane: Arsenals. Cebeci participated in all campaigns commanded by the Sultan or the Grand Vizier, and in smaller numbers in other campaigns. Cebeci were also in-charge of policing the area around the Hagia Sophia[297]. It is not known how long after 1658, Cebeci continued to wear armour or use their helmets. The Cebeci helmet clearly displays a Janissary Spoon Holder in place of the helmets' movable nose guard.

ARABACI

Arabaci: Transport Drivers formed their own permanent corps in the Standing Army. The Artillery and Infantry relied on Arabaci to transport weapons and ammunition, as well provide gun limbers – using the same cannon wagons as the Cebeci. In 1598, Arabaci had 700 Soldiers. They were organized as Boluk: Files (Sub-Regiments), typically of 100 Soldiers. Traditionally, the battlefield role of the Arabaci was to reinforce the Tabur-Cengi with specially adapted versions of the Hussite Wagenburgen: fortified wagons.

FORTIFIED WAGONS

Fortified wagons constructed for Sultan Ahmed III (who succeeded to the throne in 1703), seen in Court miniatures depicting the camp setup for his son's circumcision, are massive vehicles[298]. Mounted on four large solid wheels it is constructed like a castle wall, complete with crenellations, and mounting a smaller central tower. The wagon is painted white, and wheels yellow with black iron work. Armed with cannon, which can be seen through square ports cut into the lower half. Another miniature appears to show two smaller single-story castle wagons, one drawn by an elephant, with musketeers manning the top, and the lower portion shows small cannon firing through square ports cut into the wall. There is also a 1774 account of the Russian-Turkish War, "[Turkish oxen] … dragged some hundreds of armed … [wagons], which had been brought with a design to enclose the Russians in their … [entrenchments]."[299]

Modern history accounts state the Arabaci wagons design are missing[300]. However, one is shown in

---

294 Sakul, 2013.
295 Nicolle, 1998.
296 Ralamb, 1658.
297 Ralamb, 1658.
298 Levni, 1720.
299 Anthing, 1813.
300 Uyar, 2009.

a 1596 Court miniature of the Battle of Keresztes[301]. This shows behind a line of cannons, Janissary standing on top of a large four-wheeled cart. It is known, that the, "Turks ... made great use of four-wheeled wagons"[302]. The Arabaci wagon is shown with a waist high timber bulwark (which acted as a barrier to people climbing-up), and what appears to be additional large circular shields (with a large boss), mounted high on the side of the wagon, for added protection. This wagon is set behind the cannons, as the wagon itself was used as the limber, and ammunition carrier. The wagon provides a high platform for the Soldiers to fire from, well over the heads of other Soldiers, and Artillery in front of the wagon.

▼ **Cebeci and fortified cannon wagon.**

EARTH BAGS

A 1787 account of the Russian-Turkish War reports Turkish Infantry while constructing their entrenchments encountered the problem of flooding, this meant that they could not sufficiently dig deep enough: "They, however, supplied this defect, by filling the sacks, with which they had the precaution to provide themselves, with sand, and they served as a rampart."[303] Well known in the 18th Century, was the technique called: "epaulement, in fortification, a side-work hastily thrown up, to cover cannon or Soldiers. It is made ... of bags of earth"[304].

---

301 Topkapi, 1609.
302 Nicolle, 1995.
303 Anthing, 1813.
304 Chambers, 1728.

CHAPTER 9: RELIGIOUS OFFICIALS AND RELIGIOUS REGULATION

Centuries-old traditions of literature on Islamic legal rulings exist on the conduct of warfare; ensuring it was to be waged in accordance with the religious principle: bellum pium: pious war, or war in accordance with God's will[305]. Historical Islamic texts on warfare are known to contain rulings on Cavalry tactics, Infantry deployments, espionage and selection of encampments. One manual on warfare covered, Persian use of Cavalry, "[and] … 72 basic uses of the lance, battle formations, and the Greek, Persian, Mesopotamian, and Maghribi (North African) styles of Cavalry training."[306] Among modern historians the general view is throughout the 18th Century there was a continuation of classical military precepts due to a conservative hold over these institutions[307]. This was identified as the case, in an account from 1806 when Sultan Selim III sought to introduce European tactics and discipline into the Turkish Army,

> "found himself obstinately resisted not only by the … [Janissary] … but that powerful party in all the … Provinces who were attached to their national and religious institutions, and regarded the introduction of European customs, whether into the Army or the state, as the first step in their national ruin."[308]

> "the older corps in the past had demonstrated violent reactions to any attempts to introduce new ways which might undermine the position they had secured in … society by virtue of their monopoly of the military techniques and weapons of the past."[309]

Modern historians tend to view the military conservatism of 18th Century Turkish, in terms, "[of the] … stereotypes of religious obscurantism"[310]. The use of weapons, tactics, even the organization and appearance of the Soldiers was infused with, "religious-legal sanction"[311]. Mandatory religious regulations underlay traditional military practices, to the extent that, "the Ulema … [Religious Scholars] … perceived any kind of advance or innovation as a direct attack on Islamic law and traditions."[312] Under Sultan Mustafa III, the 1774 order to establish a new corps of Sur'atcis: Speed Manoeuvre Artillery gave this official explanation, in religious terms:

> "Even though the Imperial Arsenal is known for its perfection in the arts of war … in recent times, other states have invented and developed small, well-crafted cannon capable of rapid fire, reaching an understanding of the science through experimentation … The … State likewise wishes to organize a Company of Rapid-Fire Artillerymen, and is issuing this imperial order to that effect."[313]

It has been argued that the reason for this explanation being given was anticipation over likely controversy generated within the Government and military establishment by introducing foreign military concepts, such as the adoption in 1774 of Flying Artillery based on European models. The edict of Sultan Mustafa III reflected Islamic teachings on the conduct of warfare that justified

---

305 Aboul-Enein, 2004.
306 Scanlon, 1961.
307 Uyar, 2009.
308 Alison, 1842.
309 Shaw, 1965.
310 Aksan, 2002.
311 Levy, 1982.
312 Mazanec, 2016.
313 Aksan, 2002.

the adoption of a European Artillery model, in accordance with the principle of Mukabele-i Bi'l-Misl: permissibility of learning from one's enemy[314][315]. It appears, that there was likely a substantial body of Islamic teachings that lay down the mandatory religious regulation of traditional uniforms, weapons and tactics. The wholesale destruction of Janissary materials after 1826 meant that it is not known to the extent, or in what form the religious regulations of the traditional military organization, weapons, tactics and uniforms took; however, it is known these played a significant role:

> "Many acknowledge ... [military weakness] ... but ... at the same time acknowledge their inability to effect a reform, which nothing but a change of religion could effect ... [this] ... prevents their taking any steps to security because the fate of the Army is supposed to be decreed ... [by the will of God]"[316].

The deep connection between religion and military reform lay at the core of the political chaos of 1807, where it is said:

> "Emissaries from the Janissary Corps, unknown to the ... [Sultan] ... mingled in ... [the ranks of the Nizam-i Cedit: New Order Army troops] ... the powerful body of the Ulema ... [Religious Scholars] ... began to preach insurrection upon the ground of the ... [Sultan] ... aiming at the overthrow of the fundamental institutions of the Koran and the Empire"[317].

During the 1808 continuation of the political unrest, the Janissary revolt facing short term reversal of fortune, apparently attempted to plead for royal mercy claiming they would adopt Nizam-i Cedit: New Order Army uniforms, and even a, "European hat should the Sultan demand."[318] Commentators, at the time, criticized this political manoeuvre on the grounds, "[this] … was a scandalous idea since wearing the European hat amounted to changing one's identity. It demonstrated that the rebels had doubtful religious convictions; they would turn infidel"[319]. The clothing laws of Sultan Selim III were used to compel compliance with his reforming policy direction for society. It may well be the case that the actual source of military opposition to his rule had been over reforms to the dress and appearance rather than the 'bayonet cause celebre' in 1807. Uniforms in this period only consisted of three items: the Bork: hat, breeches and boot colour. The Bork had meaning, where an individual's status and role was displayed. Replacement of the elaborate headgear, used within the military, such as the Janissary Bork with a common 'European hat', would have meant a personal loss of status to the wearer, and fundamentally undermined any religious meaning or significance this may have had. The Janissary Bork back flap or tail is said to represent the arm sleeve of the early Turkish spiritual leader - Haji Bektash (1209 to 1271). Haji Bektash named and consecrated the Janissary, giving them their special role in society. He is said to have placed his hand of authority on the first Janissary's heads[320].

---

314 Levy, 1982.
315 Sakul, 2012.
316 Morier, 1801.
317 Alison, 1840.
318 Sakul, 2012.
319 Sakul, 2012.
320 McLean, 1818.

▲ The 74th Cemaat Janissary Orta badge showing a wooden frame tower based on tetrahedron: triangular pyramid[321]. It could have been used to send signals from; or make calls from, such as 'the daily call to pray'. An account from the Egyptian campaign of the camp crier's 'orders of the Grand Vizier for the next day operations of his Army: "Tomorrow you are to march ... Those who wish it, may now depart"[322]. It is known, Turkish military engineers regularly converted churches into mosques in captured territories[323]. Such a structure may have served this purpose as a minaret.

---

321 Sevket, 1907.
322 Morier, 1801.
323 Sakul, 2013.

CHAPTER 10: ORTA IMAM, SAKA AND MEDICAL SUPPORT

ORTA IMAM

An 1807 illustration of a Janissary Imam, possibly one belonging to an Orta, shows the only distinguishing uniform feature is use of a green Cahouk: quilted top hat with a white turban[324]. Green headgear traditionally denotes a man who has religious privileges[325]. The Orta Imam wears a long white wrap-around shirt with a red waist wrap, under a long-sleeved red coat with yellow tape trim. Blue Russian pants and red Turkish slipper shoes complete the dress. It is generally known all Janissary Orta had their own Regimental Imam[326]. At the French siege of Acre, Djezzar, the Governor, it was said: "[sent his Imam] ... among the ... towns ... [and cities of Damascus and Aleppo] ... requesting the true believers ... to rise, in order that they might overwhelm the infidels"[327]. Two Janissary Orta had a direct religious function. One of these was the 94th Cemaat, commanded by a Chief Imam, who is said to have been the Chaplain of all the Janissary Orta in Constantinople. One source says this was the 84th Cemaat, whom had an Orthodox Imam appointed[328]. There was also the 99th Cemaat Commanded by a Seyk: Bektesi Dervishes Leader[329]. In relation to the 99th Orta, it is known that from 1591, eight Bektesi Dervishes were attached to it, and on parade marched before the Agha of the Janissary in green uniform-costumes[330]. It is also said "their Senior Baba (Spiritual Master) was honoured as a Colonel ... [of the 99th]."[331]

SAKA

Saka [Sakka]: Water-Distributor had the traditional role of providing water for washing before prayers, and also accompanied Soldiers into battle and tended the wounded[332]. There was also a water carrier in the Imperial Palace, their leader being called Saka Bashi: Chief Water Carrier. A description from the Napoleonic period, lists Saka as one of the Janissary Orta Officers[333]. An 1802 description of the Saka noted: "It is a singular thing, that the business of a water carrier should afford a dress so ornamented"[334]. A 1907 illustration of a Sakka [Saka] (Porteur d'Eau): Water Carrier[335], responsible for carrying permitted water, and dispensing this for prayers, is depicted wearing an elaborate costume, and a long white loose cloth Bork: hat with a rays-shaped Spoon Holder, and tall gilt brow-band crown. Wearing elaborate shawls over a long red sleeved coat with yellow tape trim. Blue Russian pants and red Turkish slipper shoes complete the dress. Another 1907 illustration shows a Saka wearing a brown leather bell jacket with large shoulder wings, a blue collarless shirt trimmed with yellow tape and closed with small buttons. Blue Russian pants and red Turkish slipper

---

324 Sevket, 1907.
325 War Office, 2008.
326 Goodwin, 2013.
327 Camden, 1814.
328 Goodwin, 2013.
329 Nicolle, 1995.
330 Gush, 1975.
331 Goodwin, 2013.
332 Nicolle, 1995.
333 McLean, 1818.
334 Dalvimart, 1802.
335 Sevket, 1907.

shoes, along with a tall red conical Fez, and yellow striped patterned turban complete the dress. The Saka role extended to transporting the Army's drinking water:

> "establishment of ... [Saka] ... a corps selected from the ... [Janissary] ... to attend and supply the troops with water. On this service they were also constantly employed on a march. They are mounted on horses provided with bells, to the end that their approach may be known to the troops; and each horse carries two leathern sacks containing about forty gallons of water."[336]

An important religious duty, in Islamic culture is the wudu procedure for washing parts of the body using water in preparation for formal prayers. Permitted water types that can be used for ritual washing are rain, spring, sea or river water, from melting snow or hail, tank, pond or well water, if it was considered moving-water. Even though all Soldiers had a personal water canteen, this was likely seen as prohibited water. Used for dispensing permitted water, Saka carried over their shoulder a special leather water bottle, with a carry strap, brass reinforcement, and a small tap at the end[337]. A small brass handled pot used to transfer small amounts of water for ritual purification was held in one hand. The same pot is depicted in a 1714 illustration of a Saka and water transport horse, which shows a much larger version of the bottle slung over a saddle[338]. It is known that tartavans: Turkish carriages suspended between two camels, were used for carrying water by the Saka[339].

PHYSICIAN

The Standing Army traditionally had a high level of medical support. Physicians, Surgeons and hospitals were organized for campaigns. Even in the 1700s, Turkish medical organization was far more extensive and developed than European monastic hospitals and hospital orders in the same period. Janissary on campaign had access to various Court health professionals, such as the Chikikji: Bone Setter, or Physicians. At the end of the 16th Century, it is known that there were some 113 Surgeons in the Palace. It is also known that each Janissary Orta had its responsible Chief Surgeon. The Palace's Chief Physician accompanied the Sultan during wartime, and when the Sultan remained at the Palace during war, an Army: Ardu-Yu Humayum Hekimbashisi: Chief Physician of the Army was appointed, to undertake supervision of health services on campaign[340]. An illustration of the Court Chief Physician[341], shows wearing a long black coat, and large white turban, with black pointed Fez hat. Illustrated with a long silk scarf draped over the left shoulder. Scarves were commonly hung over the shoulder to allow a person to wipe their hands. It may have been used in examinations. It is possible the Physician would lay the silk scarf down as a clean place to examine their patient.

By the Napoleonic period, Turkish Surgeons and Court Physicians were still present; however, access to medical help had been considerably reduced. An English Surgeon, sent to Constantinople recalled, "[a] ... visit from Dr. Rhazi, Physician to the ... [Captain-Pasha]"; and meeting, Dr. (Signor) Bosari, a Physician to the Grand Vizier[342]. This same English Surgeon, also met other Court Medical Practitioners, specifically recalling the, "Physician to the Sultan ... the Sultan's ... Surgeon ... [and] ... the Surgeon-in-Chief to the Army, and two other Army Surgeons"[343]. Notwithstanding meeting these practitioners, the English Surgeon complained of the general neglect of the sick in the Turkish

---

336 Wittman, 1803.
337 Sevket, 1907.
338 Vanmour, 1714.
339 Wittman, 1803,
340 Sari, 2000.
341 Sari, 2002.
342 Wittman, 1803.
343 Wittman, 1803.

Army. The lack of medical support, at the provincial level military was even more poorly provided, as this account from an English Diplomat who accompanied the Turkish Army into Egypt:

> "shocking to say, every unfortunate person attacked with the disorder must trust to nature for his recovery; for no medical assistance is afforded to him. A Pasha may sometimes have a Physician in his suite; but he must either attend only upon the person of his master, or he is so ignorant of his profession as to be useless in dangerous cases. Were humanity ever to send him to the assistance of a poor sufferer, that principle would, I am afraid, soon be stifled; for, as his salary is fixed, he can have no interest in attending upon a person who is not able to repay his trouble."[344]

Seeing medical conditions on a Turkish warship, it was reported: "The place set apart for the sick was very ill calculated for that purpose; and but little attention seemed to be paid to this part ... the disregard with which the sick were treated ... [and] ... little encouragement bestowed on those who had the charge of them."[345]

▶ At night a Janissary carrying a lantern painted with the badge of the 4th Boluk Janissary Orta, accompanies a Doctor and Saka with their donkey carrying large water vessels.

FIGURE 15: Orta Imam (1750 onwards).
FIGURE 16: Saka dispensing water for prayers.
FIGURE 17: Saka wearing a bell jacket.

---

344 Morier, 1801.
345 Wittman, 1803.

CHAPTER 11: MEHTAR AND TURKISH MUSIC SOLDIERS IN EUROPEAN ARMIES

Mehtar: Music Corps were a significant development in Turkish military organization from its early beginnings. Instruments used by the Mehtar, were the:

KOS	Giant timpani	ZIL [ZIL-ZEN]	Cymbals
NAKARE	Small kettledrum	KABA ZURNA	Oboe
DAVUL	Bass drum	CEVGEN	Bell Tree

The Davul was a large side mounted base drum played by an Officer called a Bache Mehter: who was the Chief of the Bass Drums, and Second Chief of Music[346]. Boru appeared similar to a brass trumpet or a bugle with an additional oval handle fitted, so that the players' hand does not interfere with the instrument correctly vibrating (which could occur if directly holding it). Other illustrations commonly show Boru players directly holding the trumpet bell. Doing so would have the effect of muting the music coming from the instrument. There was also a similar instrument called a Borouzen: a type of early trombone, which was a long trumpet with a snake-bend in it[347]. There were several versions of Kos: giant timpani. Large Kos was carried by a camel, and the largest version by an elephant. The Cevgen: bell tree, more commonly known as the 'Jingle Johnny', developed in various forms such as a bell tree or pole bearing small, concealed bells. It is known that the Cevgen was played by the Permit Maitre: Music Master of Ceremonies[348].

Mehtar provided marching and parade music for the Army. The Janissary marching style was distinctive described as a cadence[349]. The timing rhythm of the march-cadence was 1,2,3-4, and 1,3,2-4, and at every three steps they would stop and turn both right and then left[350]. It was said, their style of walking represented dignity and caution. Rest of the Janissary would follow in a slow walk, chanting-in-time: "Kerim-Allah-Eyisun, Rahim Allah- Eyisun: Generous God, Oh Merciful God!" An English military observer in Constantinople, described military music composed of, "enormous hollow trunks, beaten by mallets, unite a heavy noise to the lively notes of little timbrels, which, accompanied with clarinets and trumpets, make a very discordant sound."[351][352] An English account described the greeting of a vessel carrying the Turkish Bashaw - an Anglicization of the title of Pasha: the Admiral and General in Egypt, in 1800, "beating of kettledrums, clashing of cymbals, and playing pipe organs"[353]. An 1802 observation stated: "Turkish military music forms a combination of the most discordant sounds"[354].

Mehtar are generally depicted in the 18th Century wearing red or green Cahouk: quilted top hat with a white turban, long white, or yellow wrap-around shirt with yellow waist wrap, under a long-wide sleeved red or turquoise coat. Red Russian pants and yellow or red Turkish slipper shoes complete the dress. The Permit Maitre is also depicted wearing a yellow patterned long coat with a buttoned

---

346 Sevket, 1907.
347 Sevket, 1907.
348 Sevket, 1907.
349 Gush, 1975.
350 Nicolle, 1998.
351 McLean, 1818.
352 Johnson, 1988.
353 Low, 1911.
354 Dalvimart, 1802.

fly-vent opened over the chest. The coat had a low collar, with cuffs folded-back revealing green lining. A gold belt closed with a double oval buckle completed the dress.

TURKISH MUSIC SOLDIERS IN EUROPEAN ARMIES

Mehtar inspired the formation of formal military bands in all the major European armies. King Sobieski's 1681 former Janissary Banner: Company is said to have had a band in the Turkish manner, that used drums played from both sides, oboes, flute and a sort of brass instrument with small flat plates that hit each other, and a type of Jewish psalterium - triangle decorated with rings play by hitting it with a stick. A 1790 portrait of John Fraser of the Coldstream Guards[355]; and 1792 illustration – "Changing the Guard at St. James's Palace"[356], illustrate how British Army Turkish Musicians were commonly Black Soldiers, "[as actual] ... Turkish Musicians were never used"[357]. The presence of Black Musicians in the 18th Century British Army is well known. However, their transition into 'Turkish Musicians' appears closely related to introduction of percussion instruments to play 'Turkish music', specifically played by Black Soldier Musicians using bass drums, cymbals and tambourines. The John Fraser portrait features a tambourine, or timbrel. An 1811 illustration shows a large iron triangle held by a Turkish Musician[358].

Turkish Musicians were part of the bands of several British Regiments between 1785, and 1837. A 1793 illustration of the Black Soldier Turkish Cymbalist in the Buckinghamshire Militia shows wearing red long sleeved high collared shell jacket with long hanging triangular corners, and a tall red conical Fez with white and yellow striped turban with tall red plume[359]. An 1811 illustration of the Duke of Gloucester's Band shows a yellow short sleeved shell jacket with folded-down collar, and long hanging triangular corners, along with an enormous round turban decorated with a giant bow and tall yellow and black plume. This group was also associated with the 3rd Regiment of Foot Guards[360]. The Foot Guards Turkish Musicians wore the red coatee with sleeves shortened to reveal the veste: waistcoat long sleeves. The Guards' headgear was a large white turban decorated with beads and red and blue ostrich feathers.

A silver collar with elaborate engraving work including a matching silver cuff can be seen in the John Fraser portrait. The collar appears engraved with a Saint George shield with flags on either side. It is recorded how the band from the Coldstream Guards, around the 1800s bought among items of clothing, spending £24.15s.2d. on silver collars for the Black Musicians[361]. Silver collars and cuffs are also clearly visible in the illustration of the British Foot Guards changing the Guard at St. James's Palace with their three Black Soldier players dressed as Turkish Musicians[362]. A silver collar, from 1784, is still retained by the Queen's Royal Hussars (which uses the kettle drums of the former 3rd Hussars). This is said to date from 1772, or possibly 1776 when the wife of Lord Southampton who commanded the 3rd Hussars, gave it to be worn by a Black Soldier who played the kettle drum. As late as 1831, Black Soldiers who were Time-Beaters for the Worcestershire Regiment were known to wear, "[a] ... silver-plated stock for the neck which opened with clasps and fastened behind"[363]. This peculiar item – the silver collar or stock, have been noted elsewhere; for instance, it can be seen

---

355 Private Collection, 1790.
356 Unknown, 1792.
357 Fryer, 1984.
358 Unknown, 1811.
359 Young, 1952.
360 Unknown, 1811.
361 Fryer, 1984.
362 Unknown, 1792.
363 Fryer, 1984.

in an engraving called: 'A Harlot's Progress'[364]. This work includes a Black child servant, wearing a feathered turban almost identical to that seen in the John Fraser portrait. Wearing a metal collar identifies her as a domestic slave, which was a common practice in 18th Century London[365].

FRENCH ARMY TURKISH MUSICIANS

An illustration of the Black Soldier 'Turkish Music' Cymbalist in Napoleon's Consular Guard, around 1801[366][367], shows an elaborate and somewhat fanciful 'Turkish' headgear, while the rest of the uniform is a conventional French Musician for the period. An 1804 French Army Black Soldier 'Turkish music' Cymbalist for the Grenadiers wore a typical Bands uniform for the period, with an elaborate 'Turkish' hat[368]. An 1811 French Army Musician shows them wearing a Mameluke-style of uniform[369]. Several Musicians' uniforms for Black Soldiers are documented from the Napoleonic period, and most of these wear variations of the French Mameluke-style of uniform developed in the French Army during this time.

▶ A 1907 illustration of the Permit Maitre: Music Master of Ceremonies, and Cevgen: bell tree, from 1750 onwards[370], showing a yellow patterned long coat with a buttoned fly-vent opened over the chest. The coat had a low collar, with cuffs folded-back revealing green lining. A gold belt closed with a double oval buckle completed the dress.

▶▶ Three 1907 illustrations of a Bache Mehter, Zil-Zen and Borouzen players[371].

---

364 Hogarth, 1732.
365 Cunnington, 1967.
366 Lapeyre, 1943.
367 Boisselier, 1959.
368 Boisselier, 1959.
369 Boisselier, 1959.
370 Sevket, 1907.
371 Sevket, 1907.

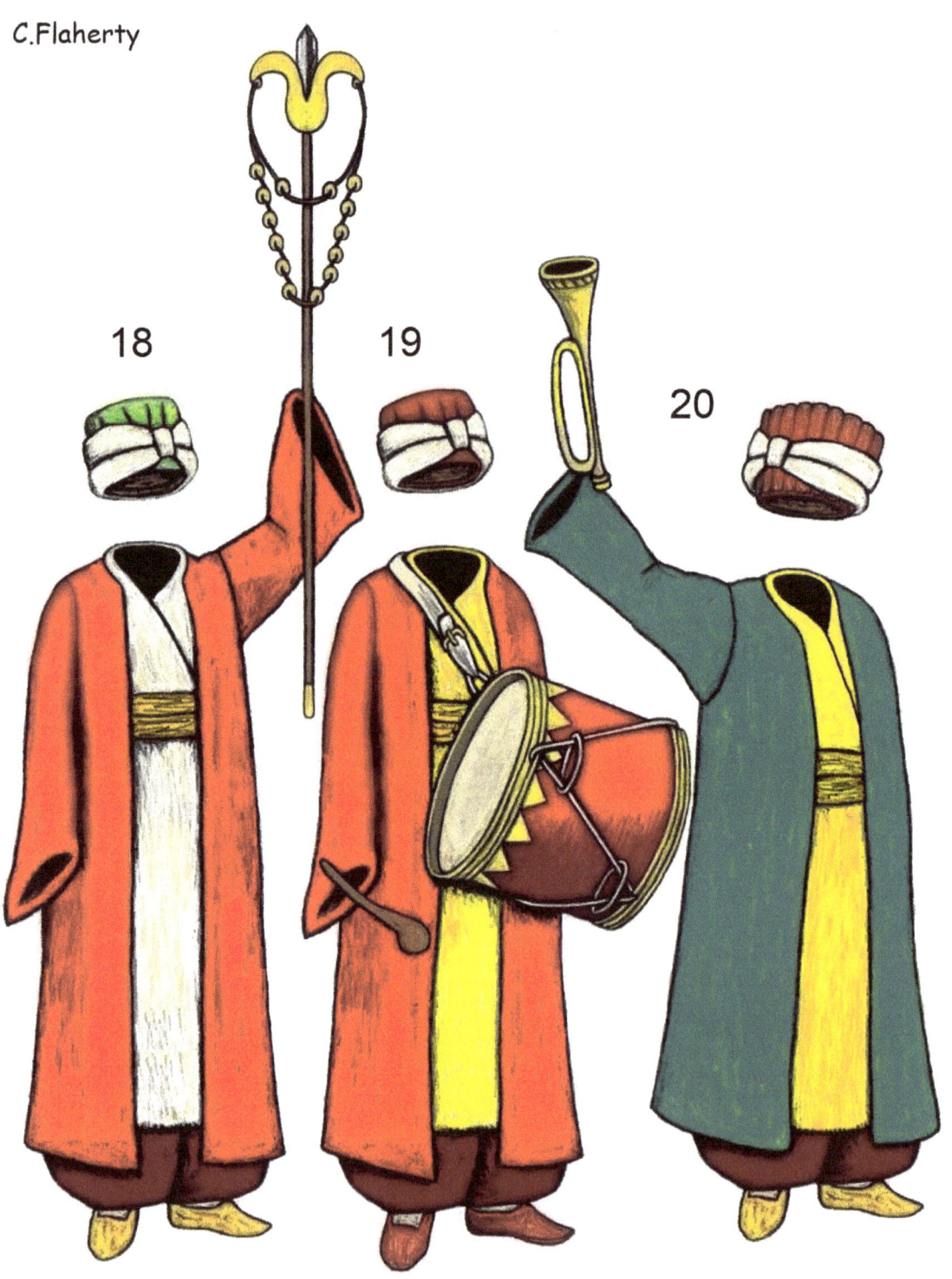

FIGURE 18: Permit Maitre: Music Master of Ceremonies, and Cevgen: bell tree.
FIGURE 19: Kos: giant timpani.
FIGURE 20: Boru: brass trumpet or a bugle.

FIGURE 21: John Fraser (1800).
FIGURE 22: Turkish Music Cymbalist and Triangle Player in the Buckinghamshire Militia (1793).
FIGURE 23: Silver collar, John Fraser portrait (1800).
FIGURE 24: Tambourine, or timbrel, John Fraser portrait (1800).
FIGURE 25: Turkish Musician's large iron triangle (1811).

FIGURE 26: Duke of Gloucester's Turkish Music Players (1811).
FIGURE 27: Black 'Turkish Music' Cymbalist in Napoleon's Consular Guard (1801).
FIGURE 28: French Army Grenadiers Black 'Turkish Music' Cymbalist's hat (1804).
FIGURE 29: French Army Musician (1811).

REFERENCES

- Aboul-Enein, Y.H. Zuhur, S. 2004 Islamic Rulings on Warfare. Carlisle, PA: Strategic Studies Institute, U.S. Army War College (October).
- Agoston, G. 2005 Guns for the Sultan: Military Power and the Weapons Industry in the Ottoman Empire. Cambridge University Press.
- Agoston, G. 2011 Military Transformation in the Ottoman Empire and Russia, 1500–1800. Kritika: Explorations in Russian and Eurasian History. Volume 12. Issue 2.
- Aksan, V. 2002 Breaking the Spell of the Baron de Tott: Reframing the Question of Military Reform in the Ottoman Empire, 1760-1830. The International History Review. Number XX. Volume 2 (June).
- Alison, A. 1842 History of Europe from the Commencement of the French Revolution in 1789, to the Restoration of the Bourbons in 1815. Volume 2. New York: Harper & Brothers.
- Alison, A. 1841 History of Europe from the Commencement of the French Revolution in 1789 to the Restoration of the Bourbons in 1815. Volume 7. Baudry, Paris.
- Alison, A. 1840 History of Europe from the Commencement of the French Revolution in 1789 to the Restoration of the Bourbons in 1815. Volume 8. Blackwood.
- Anthing, J.F. [Translator] 1813 History of the Campaigns of Count Alexander Suworow-Rymnikski. London: W. Green and T. Chaplin.
- Barbir, K.K. 2014 Ottoman Rule in Damascus, 1708-1758. Princeton University Press.
- Blackwood, W. 1841 Blackwood's Edinburgh Magazine. Volume 50.
- Boisselier, H. 1959 Negro Cymbalist in Gala Dress, 1801 (Napoleon's Consular Guard). Painting.
- Boisselier, H. 1959 Negro Cymbalist in Gala Dress, 1804 (French Grenadiers). Painting.
- Boisselier, H. 1959 Musicians, 1811. Painting.
- Borekci, G. 2006 A Contribution to the Military Revolution Debate: The Janissaries' Use of Volley Fire during the Long Ottoman-Habsburg War of 1593-1606 and the Problem of Origins. Acta Orientalia Academiae Scientiarum Hung. Volume 59. Issue 4.
- Brill, E.J. 1913 [-1936] First Encyclopaedia of Islam.
- British General Staff. 1995 [The] 1916 Handbook of the Turkish Army. Battery Press, Nashville.
- Browne, W.G. 1799 Travels in Africa, Egypt, and Syria, from the Year 1792 to 1798. London: T. Cadell (Junior), and W. Davies, Strand.
- Burckhardt, J.L. 1822 Travels in Syria and the Holy Land. London: J. Murray.
- Buyukakca, M.C. 2007 Ottoman Army in the Eighteenth Century: War and Military Reform in the Eastern European Context. Graduate Thesis. Middle East Technical University.
- Camden, T. 1814 The History of the Rise, Progress, and Overthrow of Napoleon Bonaparte. J. Stratford.
- Cavuszade, H.H. 1721 Ottoman Turks Fighting the Polish Army. Walters Manuscript.
- Chambers, E. 1728 Cyclopaedia: or, An Universal Dictionary of Arts and Sciences. Volumes 1/2. London.
- Choiseul-Gouffier, G.F.A.V. 1822 Pittoresque de la Grece. Paris: J.-J. Blaise.
- Creasy, E.S. 1878 History of the Ottoman Turks: from the Beginning of their Empire to the Present Time. London: R. Bentley.
- Cunnington, P. Lucas, C. 1967 Occupational Costume in England. A & C Black.
- Dalvimart, O. Miller, W. 1802 The Costume of Turkey: Illustrated by a Series of Engravings; with Descriptions in English and French. London: T. Bensley.
- Damurdashi, A.D. Abd al-Wahhab, B.M. 1991 Al-Damurdashi's Chronicle of Egypt, 1688-1755 [Al-Durra Al- Musana Fi Akhbar Al-Kinana]. Brill.

- Dastrup, B.L. 1992 King of Battle: A Branch History of the U.S. Army's Field Artillery. TRADOC Branch History Series.
- Diderot, D. d'Alembert, J.Le.R. 1772 Encyclopaedia.
- Douwes, D. 2000 Ottomans in Syria: A History of Justice and Oppression. I.B.Tauris.
- Elgood, R. 1995 Firearms of the Islamic World: In the Tared Rajab Museum, Kuwait. I.B.Tauris.
- Eton, W. 1798 A Survey of the Turkish Empire. London: T. Cadell and W. Davies, Strand.
- Fleet, K. Kasaba, R. 2006 The Cambridge History of Turkey. Cambridge University Press.
- Fryer, P. 1984 Staying Power: The History of Black People in Britain. Pluto Press.
- Fuccaro, N. 2016 Violence and the City in the Modern Middle East. Stanford University Press.
- Goodwin, G. 2013 The Janissaries. Saqi Books.
- Grehan, J. 2007 Everyday Life and Consumer Culture in Eighteenth-Century Damascus. University of Washington Press.
- Gush, G. 1975 Renaissance Armies: 1480–1650. PSL, UK.
- Hathaway, J. Barbir, K. 2014 The Arab Lands Under Ottoman Rule: 1516-1800. Routledge.
- Hathaway, J. 2002 The Politics of Households in Ottoman Egypt: The Rise of the Qazdaglis. Cambridge University Press.
- Henry, C. 2005 English Civil War Artillery 1642-51. Osprey Publishing.
- Herold, J.C. 2009 Bonaparte in Egypt. Fireship Press.
- Hochenleitter, L. 1788 Vorstellung der Turkischen Haupt Armee mit 80,000 Mann in Anmarsche bei Sophia in Bulgarien. Illustration.
- Hogarth, W. 1732 A Harlot's Progress. Engraving.
- Hubert, J. 1911 Organization: How Armies are Formed for War. Hard Press Publishing.
- James, W. 1826 The Naval History of Great Britain. London: Baldwin, Cradock and Joy.
- Johnson, W.E. Bell, C. 1988 The Ottoman Empire and the Napoleonic Wars. Partizan Press.
- Kelly, C. 1831 History of the French Revolution, and of the Wars. London: J. Rider.
- Knotel, R. 1890 Turkei. Janitscharen. Illustration.
- Kobell, W.A.W. 1813 [-1809] Turkish Infantry. Illustration. Artaria & Co.: Vienna.
- Lapeyre, E. 1943 1st Regiment Grenadiers-a-Pied, Musicians, Grande Tenue. Painting.
- Laking, G.F.L. 1964 Greek, or Persian 19th Century Powder Charge Pouches. Wallace Collection Catalogues: Oriental Arms and Armour. London: The Trustees of the Wallace Collection. Item 2105.
- Le Prince, J-B. 1770 Polish Janissary. Etching.
- Levni, A. 1720 Surname-i Vehbi [Book of Festival]. Topkapi Palace Library.
- Levy, A. 1982 Military Reform and the Problem of Centralization in the Ottoman Empire in the Eighteenth Century, Middle Eastern Studies. Volume 18.
- Library of Congress [The U.S.] The Daily Soup Ration, 1917. Photograph Collection.
- Low, E.B. MacBride, M. [Edited & Introduction] 1911 With Napoleon at Waterloo. London: Francis Griffiths.
- McLean, T. [John Heaviside Clark] 1818 The Military Costume of Turkey. London: Thomas McLean.
- Mackesy, P. 2013 British Victory in Egypt, 1801: The End of Napoleon's Conquest. Routledge.
- Marsigli, L.F. 1732 L'Etat Militaire de l'Empire Ottoman. Amsterdam.
- Mazanec, J. 2016 The Ottoman Empire at the Beginning of Tanzimat Reforms. Prague Papers on the History of International Relations 2.
- Mikhail, A. 2013 The Animal in Ottoman Egypt. Oxford University Press.

- Moalla, A. 2005 The Regency of Tunis and the Ottoman Porte, 1777-1814: Army and Government of a North-African Eyalet at the End of the Eighteenth Century. Routledge.
- Morier, J.P. 1801 Memoir of a Campaign with the Ottoman Army in Egypt, from February to July 1800. London: J. Debrett.
- Mugnai, B. Flaherty, C. 2015 Der Lange Turkenkrieg (1593- 1606), Volume. 2: The Long Turkish War. Soldiers & Weapons 027. Soldiershop.
- Mugnai, B. Flaherty, C. 2014 Der Lange Turkenkrieg (1953-1606). Volume 1: The Long Turkish War - Habsburgs Arrest the Ottoman Advance. Soldiers & Weapons 024. Soldiershop.
- Nicolle, D. 1995 The Janissaries. Osprey Publishing.
- Nicolle, D. 1998 Armies of the Ottoman Empire 1775-1820. Osprey Publishing.
- Nolan, C.J. 2008 Wars of the Age of Louis XIV, 1650-1715: An Encyclopedia of Global Warfare and Civilization. ABC-CLIO.
- Omer [Cabizade]. 1807 Ottoman Account.
- Ozturk, T. 2016 Egyptian Soldiers in Ottoman Campaigns from the Sixteenth to the Eighteenth Centuries. War in History. Volume 23. Issue 1.
- Phillips, R. [Editor] 1803 The Monthly Magazine, or, British Register. Volume 16. Part 2. London: J. Adland.
- Private Collection. 1790 Portrait of John Fraser of the Coldstream Guards.
- Raif, M. [Efendi] 1798 Tableau des Nouveaux Reglemens de L'Empire Ottoman. Constantinople.
- Ralamb, C. 1658 [-1657] Cebeci. Ralamb Costume Book. Royal Library in Stockholm.
- Rothenberg, G.E. 1978 The Art of Warfare in the Age of Napoleon. Indiana University Press.
- Sadat, D.R. 1972 Rumeli Ayanlari: The Eighteenth Century. The Journal of Modern History. Volume 44. Number 3 (September).
- Sakul, K. [Lenman, B.P. Editor] 2013 Military Engineering in the Ottoman Empire. Military Engineers and the Development of the Early-Modern European State. Dundee University Press.
- Sakul, K. 2012 What Happened to Pouqueville's Frenchmen? Ottoman Treatment of the French Prisoners During the War of the Second Coalition (1798-1802). Turkish Historical Review 3.
- Sakul, K. [Gonergun, F. Raina, D. Editors] 2011 General Observations on the Ottoman Military Industry, 1774- 1839. Problems of Organization and Standardization Europe and Asia: Historical Studies on the Transmission, Adoption and Adaptation of Knowledge. Springer.
- Sakul, K. 2009 An Ottoman Global Moment: War of Second Coalition in the Levant. Georgetown University Dissertation. Washington, DC.
- Sari, N. 2000 The Medical Organization at the Ottoman Court. Studies in History of Medicine & Science. Volume XVI. Numbers 1-2.
- Sari, N. Erke, U. 2002 Chief Physician of Ottoman Court. 38th International Congress on History of Medicine, Turkish Medical History Through Miniature Pictures Exhibition. Istanbul.
- Scalenghe, S. 2014 Disability in the Ottoman Arab World, 1500-1800. Cambridge University Press.
- Scanlon, G.T. [Editor and Translator] 1961 Umar Ibn Ibrahim Al-Awasi al-Ansari: Tafrij al-Qurub fi Tadbir al- Hurub [A Muslim Manual of War]. Cairo: American University at Cairo Press.
- Scott, W. 1827 The Life of Napoleon Bonaparte. Volume VI. Paris: A. and W. Galignani.
- Sevket, M. [Mahmoud Chevket Pasha] 1907 L'Organization et les Uniformes de l'Armee Ottomanne. Premiere Partie.
- Shaw, S.J. 1965 The Nizam-i Cedid Army Under Sultan Selim III 1789-1807. Oriens. Volumes 18/19 (1965/1966).
- Siborne, W. 1848 The Waterloo Campaign, 1815 (4th Edition). A. Constable, Westminster.

- Sunar, M.M. 2006 Cauldron of Dissent: A Study of the Janissary Corps, 1807-1826. Binghamton University Dissertation.
- Topkapi [Palace Museum]. 1526 Sultan Suleiman during the Battle of Mohacs. Painting. Istanbul.
- Topkapi [Palace Museum]. 1609 Mezokeresztes, 1596. Turkish Miniature. Hazine. Istanbul.
- Tyrrell, F. H. 1910 Old Turkish Military Costumes and Standards. The Imperial and Asiatic, Quarterly Review and Oriental and Colonial Record. Third Series. Volume XXX. Numbers 59 & 60 (July-October).
- Unknown. 1792 Changing the Guard at St. James's Palace. Illustration. Anne S.K. Brown Military Collection. BDR: 228707.
- Unknown. 1805 [-1600] Ein Gemeiner Janitschar in Egypten (Dated 1805). Illustration. Vinkhuijzen, H.J. [Collection]. New York Public Library [The]. Image ID: 416264.
- Unknown. 1805 [-1600] Ein Janitsar in Voller Rustung [Ein Tanitfar in Voller Ruftung] (Dated 1805). Illustration. Vinkhuijzen, H.J. [Collection]. New York Public Library [The]. Image ID: 416268.
- Unknown. 1805 [-1600] Turkisch Kaiserliche Artillerie (Dated 1788). Illustration. Vinkhuijzen, H.J. [Collection]. New York Public Library [The]. Image ID: 416254.
- Unknown. 1811 Duke of Gloucester's Band: Ensemble Associated with the 3rd Regiment of Foot Guards. Illustration.
- Unknown. 1817 [-1810] Soldier of Turkish Artillery (Hand Dated 1817). Illustration. Vinkhuijzen, H.J. [Collection]. New York Public Library [The]. Image ID: 416318.
- Unknown. 1830 Fighting at the Gates of Algiers. Print Illustration.
- Uyar, M. Erickson. E.J. 2009 A Military History of the Ottomans: From Osman to Ataturk. ABCCLIO.
- Valentini, G.W. [Anonymous Translator] 1828 Military Reflections on Turkey. C. & J. Rivington: London.
- Vanmour, J-B, Scotin, G. (Engraver) 1714 Saka, Charitable Derviche Qui Porte de l'Eau Par la Ville et la Donne par Charite [Saka, Charitable Dervish Who Carries Water Through the City and Gives it Out of Charity]. L. Cars, Paris. Illustration. New York Public Library [The]. Image ID: 94402.
- Walsh, T. 1803 Journal of the Late Campaign in Egypt. Cadell & Davies, Strand, London.
- War Office [The]. (2008) 1915 Notes on the Turkish Army: With a Short Vocabulary of Turkish Words and Phrases. N & M Press.
- Watts, R.D. 1997 The Ottoman Army of the 18th Century. Agema Publications.
- Watts, W. Mayer, L. 1806 Camp at Daub-Pascia. Illustration. Anne S.K. Brown Military Collection. BDR: 233584.
- Wellington, A.W. [Gurwood, J. Editor] 1844 The Dispatches of Field Marshal the Duke of Wellington, During His Various Campaigns in India, Denmark, Portugal, Spain, the Low Countries, and France. Volume 4. Parker, Furnivall & Parker, London.
- Winter, M. 2003 Egyptian Society Under Ottoman Rule, 1517-1798. Routledge.
- Wittman, W. 1803 Travels in Turkey, Asia-Minor, Syria, and Across the Desert into Egypt During the Years 1799, 1800, and 1801, in Company with the Turkish Army, and the British Military Mission. London: Richard Phillips.
- Yener, E. 2017 Small Copper and Bass Oval Disk Engraved With the Word: Janissary in Ottoman. Private Collection.
- Yener, E. 2016 Ottoman Seapower and Naval Technology During Catherine II's Turkish War 1768-1792. International Naval Journal. Volume 9.
- Yildiz, G. [Editor] 2013 Osmanli Askeri Tarihi: Kara, Deniz ve Hava Kuvvetleri 1792-1918 [Ottoman Military History: Land, Sea and Air Forces 1792-1918]. Istanbul.
- Young, W. Edwards, F. 1952 [-1793] Cymbalist, Buckinghamshire Militia. Painting. Anne S.K. Brown Military Collection. BDR: 247018.

OTHER TITLES BY THE SAME AUTHOR

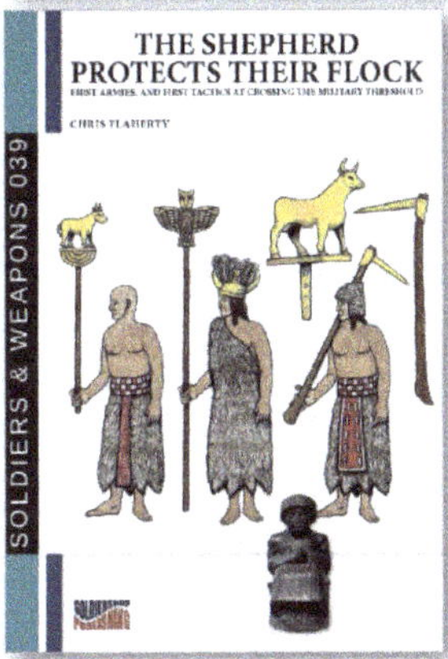

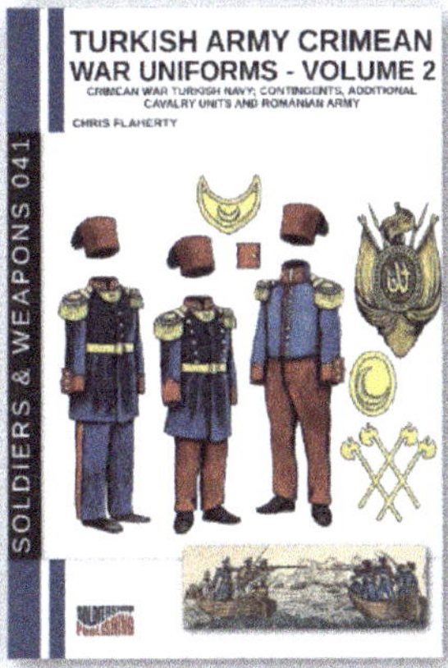

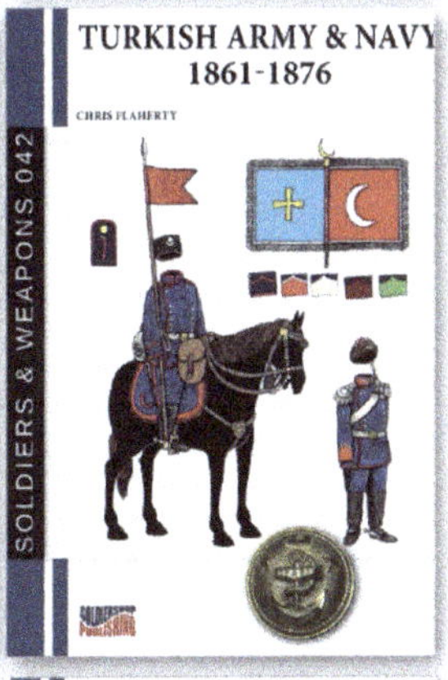

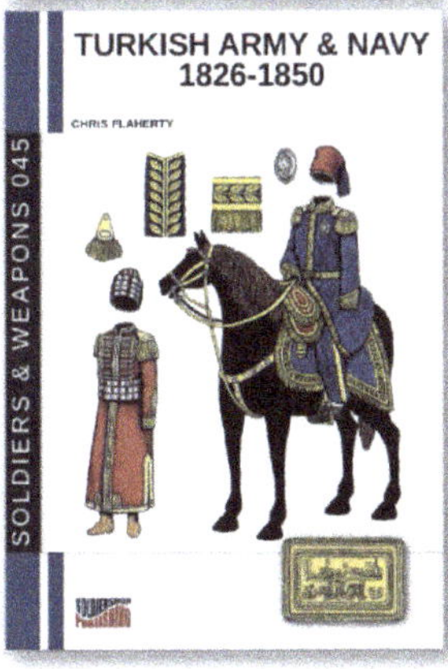

SOLDIERS & WEAPONS 054